Finding a Voice

Finding a Voice

Men, Women, and the
Community of the Church

Mark Pryce

SCM PRESS LTD

0 334 02662 8

For my brothers and sister
Neil, Paul, and Kathryn

First published 1996
by SCM Press Ltd
9-17 St Albans Place, London N1 0NX

Typeset at Regent Typesetting, London,
and printed in Great Britain by
Biddles Ltd, Guildford and King's Lynn

Contents

Acknowledgments

I would like to thank the individuals and groups who have helped me in the writing of this book, and especially those who have contributed material to the project and helped to refine ideas. Much of what is written here has arisen out of innumerable conversations; I am grateful for those dialogues and hope that they will continue. In this connection I owe particular thanks to Patrick Moore, James B. Nelson, George Bush, Philip Bowen, Lee Bowen, Donald Reeves, Philip Sheldrake, Alex Shepard, Michael Bourke and his group, Morris Williams, Martin Roper, Miriam Byrne and Hamish Good.

My interest in Men's Studies was launched with the invitation to write a *Contact* Pastoral Studies Monograph in the area, and I am grateful to Stephen Pattison and the editorial board of *Contact* for that opportunity. The meditation 'Touching in the Sea' was written for the Student Christian Movement's journal *Movement*. I am grateful for the perspectives of the World Council of Churches on the community of men and women in the church, which were introduced to me by the Delhi Brotherhood Society, and for the hospitality and contacts they offered me on my visit to their city. My thanks also to Christopher Howe and Mark Warner for their technical help.I am especially grateful to those have read parts of the text and commented upon it in its various evolutionary stages: Leslie Houlden, John Bowden, Sally Leeson, Matt Thompson, Paul Beattie, Margaret Lydamore, Penny Rose-Casemore, and, finally, James Woodward, whose generous support and encouragement have been invaluable.

Introduction:

Listening to the Voice of This Book

I believe poetry must … find its voices in the byways, laneways, backyards, nooks and crannies of self … It is critics who talk of an 'authentic voice'; but a poet, living his uncertainties, is riddled with different voices, many of them in vicious conflict. The poem is the arena where these voices engage each other in open and hidden combat, and continue to do so until they are all heard. If there is an 'authentic voice' it is found in the atmosphere deliberately created so that the voices of uncertainties may speaksing their individual stories. The imagination, so often interpreted in terms of hierarchy, insists on its own democracy. (Brendan Kennelly)[1]

Listening, responding and acknowledging one another's truth ought to be the basis of all truly ecumenical dialogue. Through it, we would be led to repent of our separation from one another … we would be released from our fears into a partnership in which we nourish one another in a mutual, ecumenical ministry.   (Pauline Webb)[2]

A young man asks to come and see me. He says he needs to talk but does not want to. He arrives and sits down. Then he barely says a word. His physical presence speaks with one voice, and his tense silence with another. Gradually he unwinds, but in a way which is very painful for him. The more he opens up, the more he wants to run away. It seems the problem is that he is lonely, but not obviously so. He has mates, a group, a lifestyle; but 'inside' he feels alone, unloved, dissatisfied. What he seems to be saying when he is with the crowd – that he is successful and self-sufficient – is not what he wants to say. Yet what he wants to say he cannot, because he is afraid. He does not ever speak the language of fear, but it is all there waiting to pour out. He wants a partner, someone to cherish him, and yet that scares him, so he 'uses' people – or tries to. He is an expert in computers, and spends time on the internet 'meeting people'. This concerns him. He feels that he might be hiding away, living a life in virtual reality. But there is no pressure on him in that world of the screen. With technology, he is fully in control – so much so that he can say things about himself that he would never say elsewhere, face to face, or even over the 'phone. On the internet he can manage to talk of feelings all the way around the world: gauged self-disclosure. In his slick way he is reaching out, expressing need in an electronic language which keeps him safe. Different voices; ambiguous voices. He is trying to find a place in which his voices can speak. He is risking dialogue.

My aim in this book is to foster dialogue between women and men, and among men themselves – between themselves and within themselves. The book is attemping to find what Brendan Kennelly has called an 'authentic voice', which is the creation of a parliament of voices, some which are complementary, and some which contradict. These voices are both personal and social. When they speak of masculinity, they speak of men's lives: not as a subject which is separate from men as they are, but as a matter which is integrally bound up with who I am and who men are in relation with women and one another. So there will be ambiguities and conflicts: the book is a book of different voices, not of a single, universal voice: the voice of dialogue. This voice is not speaking a systematic theology, but enabling a theological reflection on some of what the multiplicity of men's voices are saying and not saying.

I hope that this dialogue will be ecumenical, that is, part of the reconciling work of the church, seeking peace and justice and the integrity of creation. Through dialogue this peace begins, as partners come to recognize the human dignity of each person, even their own dignity, shaped by gender, race and sexual orientation. Dignity is not ours despite these, but is ours because of them: they are our humanness, and should be cherished and celebrated as such. I hope that men's reconsideration of their masculinities will contribute to the coming of justice for the whole human community as it enables men to hear the differing voices within themselves and among themselves, and to hear the voices of women. Men cannot find freedom alone.

This book accepts the voices of feminism as an opportunity for men to re-shape their own self-understanding. In suggesting that women have assumed a prophetic voice, in Chapters 1 and 2 I encourage men to learn from women, to explore the anxieties which lurk behind the power structures and processes of patriarchy, and to accept that abusive gender regimes are harmful for men as well as women. Chapters 3, 4 and 5 set out some of the literature and ideas of the men's movement, exploring issues concerning men whilst also seeking critically to examine them and the variety of solutions which they presented. Then the limitations and creative possibilities of masculine theology are explored as the book works towards a new ecumenical vision in which difference in gender and sexuality is celebrated and the church's ancient fears of sexual and erotic ambiguity are laid aside. A final chapter of meditations focuses on the sexual, gendered nature of human being as it is embodied in the person of Jesus Christ and experienced through salvation, tracing connections between religious belief, sexual desire and gender identity.

1

On Learning from Women

Prophecies of the disputed guest

There is a story which is told in all four Gospels: the story of the woman who anoints Jesus. It is a story designated as especially sacred: 'Truly, I say to you, wherever this gospel is preached in the whole world, what she has done will be told in memory of her' (Mark 14.9; also Matthew 26.13) . In both the Gospels of Mark and Matthew this anointing takes place at Bethany, in the house of Simon the leper. It is a story told at the very beginning of the passion narrative: the anointing of Jesus by the woman is his anointing for suffering and death, with symbolism of specific reference to burial. In Mark Jesus is eating a meal when the woman comes into the house. The woman is portrayed as an intruder – she breaks into the intimacy of a meal shared with his disciples and closest admirers. One may imagine, with historical plausibility, that all the diners are men. The intrusive woman is not a welcome guest, for when she pours expensive oil over the head of Jesus his disciples are indignant at the extravagance of her actions. They dispute what she has done. Her actions make them angry. They are angry with the woman, angry within themselves. She has wasted the ointment! It should have been sold and the money distributed, put to good use! The disciples are blind to the beauty in what she has done – to them it is indulgence, an affront, unethical, an error. The woman has done an outrageous act which discounts the needs of the poor.

The disciples have not understood the truth which the woman's action reveals: that Jesus is the Anointed One, the Christ. The woman who has come in from outside has proclaimed the gospel of a messiah who comes to serve and to suffer and to die. The unwanted guest reveals among the disciples what they had yet to apprehend. In anointing the Christ she has demonstrated the hidden purposes of God. Wherever the gospel is preached, those who hear it are to remember the prophecy and faithfulness of the woman who anointed the Saviour. For the woman's outrageous gesture is the gateway in the narrative to Christ's paschal self-offering. Her doing the beautiful thing of the anointing reveals the hidden truth and initiates the healing work of Christ.

In Luke's Gospel the story is told differently and placed earlier in the narrative (7.36–50). Jesus is at a meal in the house of Simon the Pharisee. The woman who anoints him is called an outsider, a 'sinner'. She comes into the house from the city and stands behind Jesus, at his feet, weeping, wetting his feet with her tears and drying them with her hair and kissing them in humility and devotion. In Luke's version it is the feet of Jesus which the woman anoints, not his head. And the host is appalled by the woman's touching of Jesus – shocked that Jesus can allow such a woman, a sinner, to handle his feet at table. For Simon, the anointing – the woman's touch – has brought the identity of Jesus into question: 'If this man were a prophet, he would have known who and what sort of woman this is who is touching him, for she is a sinner' (Luke 7.39). The woman, and Jesus' interaction with her, have disturbed the faith of this sincere and devout man.

Yet what seems to undo divine order is where divine generosity is played out. For this outrageous act of the sinful woman exposes the meanness of the Pharisee and brings the woman forgiveness and peace. For the woman who was uninvited is so much more generous and hospitable towards Christ than his host who does not know either his duty towards his guest or, implicitly, his need of God, and so cannot welcome the generosity of God embodied in Christ. The man who offers Jesus his house and table does not welcome in his heart, not knowing within himself what the woman wholly relies upon : the loving nature of God.

Then turning towards the woman he said to Simon, 'Do you

see this woman? I entered your house; you gave me no
water for my feet, but she has bathed my feet with her tears
and dried them with her hair. You gave me no kiss, but from
the time I came in she has not stopped kissing my feet. You
did not anoint my head with oil, but she has anointed my
feet with ointment. Therefore, I tell you, her sins, which
were many, have been forgiven; hence she has shown great
love. But the one to whom little is forgiven, loves little'
(Luke 7.44–47).

The woman's ointment and tears act like chemicals: they
bring the gospel suddenly to light, making it visible – the presence and action of God's love and forgiveness and welcome
in Christ. It is the anointing woman, the intruder, who reveals
Christ to the religious man who despises her, the man who has
patronized his guest. It is she who is saved though she was not
invited, who by her tears and touch brings to the surface the
grace of God which the man of God had not apprehended.

In both versions of the anointing story the un-named
woman is the outsider, the intruder whom men observe and
assess, and of whom they disapprove. In both versions of the
story Jesus endorses what the woman has demonstrated; she
reveals that the purposes of God's healing intentions are not to
be contained within the established expectations of the disapproving men who gaze at her, and in their gazing believe
that they control the purpose and meaning of her actions. The
anointing woman is the purifier and reformer of perverse
religion and misunderstanding: she rescues Christ from these
misapprehensions. The woman outsider subverts the religion
that is understood to be the norm, and through Jesus'
responses to her actions, she who was designated as *other*, as
an outsider, becomes the location and exemplar for the workings of divine grace. Jesus – whom his disapproving host
regards as a spectacle – is indeed exposed: as the anointed
victim, Saviour, the chosen of God manifested in marginality,
the one whose identity now becomes strange and difficult and
an issue of shame. In Luke's version of the story the Pharisee's
dinner party ends in the confusion of a disturbing question:

But those who were at table with him began to say amongst themselves, 'Who is this who even forgives sins?' (Luke 7.49).

Another disputed guest: the prophecies of Virginia Woolf

> When a subject is highly controversial – and any question about sex is that – one cannot hope to tell the truth. One can only show how one came to hold whatever opinion one does hold. One can only give one's audience the chance of drawing their own conclusions as they observe the limitations, the prejudices, the idiosyncracies of the speaker. Fiction here is likely to contain more truth than fact.[1]

Virginia Woolf, introducing *A Room Of One's Own*, her essay on women's writing which began in October 1928 as talks to the scholars of Girton College and Newnham College, Cambridge, re-invents herself. In writing about writing, Woolf the writer writes a fiction: she assumes a shifting identity, becomes not one woman writer but many, a range of characters and voices – 'Call me Mary Beton, Mary Seton, Mary Carmichael or by any name you please.' In this fiction, in the imaginary few days preceding her talks, Virginia Woolf imagines her new self sitting on the banks of a river in a city called Oxbridge preparing what she has to say to women scholars about women's writing. Oxbridge is a university city, *the* university city, the place which represents education, learning, literary tradition; a place for the writing of books, books which are read and approved as worthy of study and argument, of contradiction or canonization. Oxbridge is the place of scholarship fostered by economic security and social acceptance, where minds are trained for leadership in industry, commerce, government, the professions. It is a place exclusively for men, a university made up of wealthy colleges endowed over generations for the education of men and not women.

So from the river bank the woman writer rises and walks across a college lawn, to be shouted at by a porter for trespassing on the preserve of the male dons and male scholars.

She tries to gain admittance to a college library to consult a
manuscript, but is refused reader's privileges until she has a
letter of introduction or is accompanied by a Fellow of the
college: as a woman in Oxbridge she needs the good offices of
a man. She admires the ancient splendour of a college chapel,
its soaring architecture and shimmering glass, and hears the
thunder of its organ music, and longs to be inside but feels she
must not, that she is unqualified, unwelcome – as a woman –
to be there in her own right. She is invited to enjoy a very
splendid lunch at a rich and venerable college, a men's college,
and then a supper on the margins of the city, where the
women's college is: a supper meagre in culinary comparison,
served by an institution still seeking acceptance in Oxbridge, a
women's college underfunded in a university made wealthy
by male donors, a college barely esteemed in an academic
world crowded with the knowledge and writings of men.

Reflecting on these differences the woman writer begins to
see her disadvantage in relation to the privilege of men. She
begins to understand that for hundreds of years women have
been daughters and wives, the possessions of men, not
owners of property or endowers of colleges. Women have
been mothers and nurses and housekeepers, largely confined
to the home in roles for which an education in Oxbridge has
been thought unnecessary and inappropriate, and so they
have written little, kept busy with other duties. Wandering
around the luxury and tranquillity of the university, realizing
the privacy which men enjoy in their colleges, the woman
writer begins to understand how much more women have yet
to enjoy in their own sparse places of learning so newly
established. The woman writer begins to understand that her
literary sisters through the ages have been largely smothered
and buried and busied into silence, and that like them she is
barred from a place in which she might set about finding a
voice: 'how unpleasant it is to be locked out ... how it is worse
perhaps to be locked in ... thinking of the safety and pros-
perity of the one sex and the poverty and insecurity of the
other ... of the effect of tradition and of the lack of tradition on
the mind of a writer ... '[2] The place of privilege is a place where

writing can be done, but it may also be a prison. Women are excluded from this dangerous place of creativity; they have no history of speaking and writing out of which to speak.

The day in Oxbridge, a day on the outside, a day locked out of the libraries and chapels and the benefits of colleges, teaches the woman writer what it is that women require in order to write. Women require what men already enjoy: financial security and the necessary physical and personal space: 'a woman must have money and a room of her own if she is to write'.[3] A woman must have the means to be independent and critical: 'five hundred a year stands for the power to contemplate ... a lock on the door means the power to think for oneself'.[4]

It would be a thousand pities if women wrote like men, or lived like men, or looked like men, for if two sexes are quite inadequate, considering the vastness and variety of the world, how should we manage with only one?[5]

When women have these things which men enjoy and they are more free to write, they will not write as men do. Women must 'be themselves'. They must write as women. They must find a voice which is authentic, which expresses their experiences as women and the perspectives which arise from those experiences. Women will no longer be only the subjects of literature, there to be written about by men, but will write for themselves about themselves. Women will write their own fictions which will displace the fictions of men so that these fictions may be understood as such. Women writers will expose the fictions of men as limited and limiting. Women will write as those who have been overlooked by men; they will see what men have failed to see. Women writers will write the 'infinitely obscure lives' of women which men do not record, the hidden domestic lives of women who are mothers, daughters, housekeepers, the lives of the women workers in the factories, shops and streets. Women will write down their inner worlds about which most men have not known or understood. Women will begin to describe what men are not able to see for themselves; they will write of male 'vanities' and 'peculiarities'. The fiction of women will tell the truth about men; a task of the woman writer is to be 'very brave and very honest', to 'go behind the other sex and tell us what she found there', to find that 'spot the size of a shilling at the back of the head which one can never see for oneself'.[6] Women will describe these hidden things, they will expose them. This is a work of completion, a contribution to our knowing something of the human whole.

Which is not to say that women writers are to become obsessed with themselves once they have what they need to enable them to write. Women are to be true to themselves, to their experience, but not in ways which hamper or diminish them. They are to have confidence in themselves, to be open-minded and bold. They are not to defer to the tendencies of literary orthodoxy, nor are they to be intimidated by the business of ranking books as 'worthless' or 'great'. Women are to write what they wish to write, avoiding fruitless arguments about merit or superiority. Women are to write in such a way as to supersede the limitations placed on them. They are to be encouraged in those freedoms and opportunities which have already been gained, and to go on beyond the boundaries of sex, to be like Coleridge or Shakespeare in their fertile imaginations. And though they lack the fullness of what they may need, they are not to be silent. The woman writer is to write, to let the poet be born in her. Even in poverty and obscurity she must write.

Virility has now become self-conscious.[7]

Even as Virginia Woolf wrote down the words she spoke to the scholars of Newnham and Girton, it was happening. The woman writer was addressing women scholars. Though poor in comparison with men's colleges and still not accepted as full members of the universities in Oxford or Cambridge, even so, women's colleges were being founded. In universities such as London and Edinburgh women were studying, analysing, experimenting, writing; women were finding self-expression in ever more various and powerful ways. There were more and more women's voices. Through education women were gaining the qualifications for entry to the hallowed institutions and professions which once were the preserve of exclusively-educated men. Women had the vote, and had largely gained it for themselves against severe resistance. Women could own property in their own right and were ceasing to be the property of men. Through artificial contraception women were gaining control of fertility and reproduction, and this basic physical freedom became the ground for other freedoms to grow. Women were beginning to encroach on that which was forbidden them, on that which was the preserve of men.

So it seemed to Virginia Woolf, to the woman writer, that as women acquired the means to create new fictions of their own, fictions which they would write rather than merely receive from men, the men who wrote made fictions which were wholly for themselves, fictions of strong and isolated men – the heroes of Kipling and Galsworthy – which had no appeal and gave no nourishment to women.[8] These were superficial stories to shore up a crumbling patriarchal culture. They were writings which avoided the demands and desires of the feminine, even the feminine within the men themselves. And as the women, though still for the main part outside the colleges and professions and board-rooms and governments, seemed more and more to encroach upon the territory of men, so more and more the men would seek to exclude them, their resistance fuelled with a rage which was violent, thorough, ruthless and irrational – a rage which found its ultimate expression in Fascism and brutal dictatorship, in Mussolini's Italy and Hitler's Germany, though its roots crept into every family and institution where men were dominant, and where it might lurk beneath fictions of tradition, science or moral decency.

In her *Three Guineas*, Woolf takes as a prime example of this fear of women their exclusion from the ordained ministry in the church, a church which is itself a patriarchal fiction, an utter rewriting of Christ's intention and original practice. Holy Orders were a fiction written by men to exclude women through a professionalization of ministry which required male gender as a qualification. From the apostolic age onwards women were so diminished in status by hierarchy that they were almost of no account within the churches, allowed only into the margins of ministry and deemed worthy of only minimal pay for their work as deaconesses.[9] But Woolf sees this marginality of women in the structures of men as a source of power. She sees that women can bring about transformation as they realize their lack of inclusion, the absence of involvement, investment and benefit for women in the existing culture of men. By consciously including themselves as members of the 'Society of Outsiders',[10] women will seek new words and ways of being and working. Virginia Woolf suggests that on the outside is a powerful place to be. She gives as an example of women's power to disturb the *status quo* the concern being expressed by the clergy, the male clergy, at the trend of women absenting themselves from church. In particular, she quotes the anxiety and alarm among senior clergy as they note the reluctance of young women being educated at the new Oxbridge colleges to involve themselves in the institutional churches. Hence, Woolf suggests, the Church of England has been driven to establish a Commission on the Ministry of Women. Hence its remarkable findings, an admission that there is no rational or theological barrier to women receiving the grace of holy orders. Hence, it seems to the woman writer, women have the power to rewrite the institutional fictions of the church from outside its sanctuaries and sacred orders. For Virginia Woolf, this is a sign:

> those also serve who remain outside. By making their absence felt their presence becomes desirable. What light this shows upon the power of outsiders to abolish or modify other institutions of which they disapprove ... [11]

From the outside in

Whether the ordination of women to the priesthood in the Church of England is a sign of women's power and genuine inclusion in the church is an issue which is still contended. For some it is clearly the case that women now have authority within the church, and so enjoy an equal place with men to serve, and to serve in ways which are true to themselves as women. At last women may exercise their special gifts within the church. Others lament the day when women were 'priested' for the first time. In their view, that day saw the inclusion of women in a hierarchical and patriarchal establishment which is the antithesis in theology and practice of all that women seek in an authentic Christian community: women have become captive to male structures by so endorsing them and participating in them.

Virginia Woolf was herself deeply ambivalent towards Holy Orders. No doubt her ambivalence was influenced by her experience of the ways in which the clergy of her day practised the ministries implied in those orders. Yet she perceived in the slow movement of the Church of England towards a shift in understanding the nature and role of women in relation to those Holy Orders a sign of women's power to bring about change from 'the outside', change in favour of those who are 'shut out', the power of transformation.

Some sixty or seventy years after Woolf wrote *A Room Of One's Own*, women have achieved a great deal through feminism, the women's movement and the campaigns for women's rights of which Woolf was a pioneer. Now there are women professors, judges, managing directors, parliamentary representatives, editors, authors; women hold positions which challenge the order of male supremacy that Virginia Woolf knew and exposed in her writing. Women may choose their own sexual partners, they may marry or not marry whomever they choose, and choose when and with whom they will make love; they may not be forced to have sex against their will, by their husbands or anyone else. Now women may control their own fertility; they have equal rights under the law and equal access to health-care, education and social services. Women may work and be paid and taxed on equal terms with men. Almost every career and professional role is open to women now. Great advances have been made for women. There is still much to be done, but much has been achieved – even the admission of women to Holy Orders in the Church of England.

It may well be that the priesting of women *is* representational of a shift in the social roles and status of women. It may be that the priesting of women gives expression to other changes within the Christian community. For as the social role of women has expanded, as women gain in self-definition, in professional and economic status, so the churches have developed ecclesiologies and theologies in response to these changes. The biblical texts have been re-interpreted, read with eyes wearing different spectacles; one might even say that the Christian *fictions* have been rewritten to include women, rewritten by women as well as by men. A great deal of attention has been paid to Jesus' treatment of women, for example, and it has been newly recognized that the New Testament texts bear witness to the inclusion of women in the ministry and mission of Christ and to their integral role in the early churches. It is now significant for believers that women were amongst the close associates of Jesus, that they were his disciples and supporters, ministered to his needs, stayed with him when the men abandoned him, and were the first to experience the empty tomb and the risen Christ. It is understood by some that Jesus of Nazareth forged a new kind of relations with the women of his time – that he was a transgressor of the social and religious boundaries which separated women from men, that his teaching and healing were equally for women as for men and that his inauguration of the Kingdom of God promises equality and freedom for women and men in a transformed community. That St Paul amply endorses these insights in the first churches of Greece and Asia Minor can no longer be comfortably overlooked by many readers of the New Testament.

Listening to the voices of women

The inclusion of women with men in a group or organization does not necessarily ensure that their participation will be welcomed or made easy. There are increasing numbers of women in management roles, particularly in middle-management, yet research into the management styles of men in secular organizations has shown that women can be marginalized and silenced even in those processes which are supposed to include them. Where women have positions of responsibility, their male colleagues and seniors may pursue strategies which aim to 'silence' them. Women may be present at meetings, they make contributions, but men choose not to hear what they have to say. It may even be that men frustrate women in their attempts to speak or make their proper contribution. The work of the sociologist Jeff Hearn suggests that these strategies operated by male managers may be understood as 'normal' male behaviour, as typically male management styles, and yet their impact is to marginalize and even to intimidate women. Psychological evaluations of men's behaviour in mixed-gender groups and management teams reveal certain common ways of behaving, such as 'hogging the show', over-assertiveness, listening only to oneself, avoiding feelings, put-downs and one-upmanship, speaking for others, interrupting, ignoring women as they speak, and so on.[12] This conduct is sometimes connected with angry, aggressive, abusive and manipulative behaviour on the part of male managers who are seeking to control women. The presence of women as managers and members of the boards and committees of an organization does not necessarily signify an inner disposition on the part of men within that organization to receive the contribution of their women colleagues or to co-operate with them.

Yet inclusion implies participation, and participation leads to transformation. This is what women are working to make real within organizations and structures. It is what men are finding hard to receive, what they fear and want to resist. Men have been seeking to have the inclusion of women in the churches on their own terms. Anglican women may be priests and deacons in the Church of England, but not yet bishops. In the Church in Wales they may be ordained as deacons only. The report on the ministry of women in the Methodist Church in Britain, *A Cry Of The Beloved*, reveals that although women have been ordained to ministry for years, yet they are still not participating fully in the life of the church at a senior level.[13] And whilst John Paul II's 'Letter to Women', written for the 1995 World Conference on Women in Beijing, seeks to include women as essential and vital to the very fabric and nature of the human and Christian community, his definition of women's roles, identity and purpose restricts the participation of women within those communities. The 'genius of women' is to be found in women's capacity to serve others, but this service is to be confined to ways which are in keeping with the God-given 'essential nature' of women and men. Women are thanked for their contributions as mothers, wives, daughters and sisters, as nuns and as workers, and the 'Letter' makes an appeal for their dignity and freedom to be fully realized, and for growth in understanding that womanhood and manhood are complementary: men and women need one another to be fully human. But this complementarity implies a radical difference between women and men, and suggests that the two are intended by God to fulfil different roles and functions. In particular, that form of Christian service characterized by the ministerial priesthood is not open to women, but only to men.[14] At the recent Synod on the Religious Life in Rome women religious were affirmed as a rich blessing to the life of the church, and yet they were excluded as full participants in the deliberations – even though they form the majority of those concerned with the issues discussed and agreed upon. This is also the case with biblical interpretation which seeks to 're-instate' women as members of the human race, co-equal with men in their essential being, but distinct from men in identity and role – obedient partner, mother, helpmate, wife, the one who 'receives', is passive, sensitive, supportive – and exclusively so.[15]

Yet what Virginia Woolf would have us look for in the ordi-nation of women is the power of 'the outsider' to transform the institution of the church. In this perspective, it is not so much the simple inclusion of women that men fear, but the transformation which they will bring about. This transforma-tion which Virginia Woolf describes with such energy and purpose may not be an easy experience for men, and she suggests that it will give rise to violent fury within them and to a defensive re-writing of men's roles and self-understanding. Men have lived for generations by the fictions which the women writers are re-writing. The new fictions are strange for men, they may even be painful. It is not easy for us to hear the voices of women, particularly if they articulate what challenges us. To listen to women is to risk change and even transformation. Because of this, men are not necessarily comfortable learning from women, even though we are reliant upon women from the very beginning. We are first taught life in our mother's body, then by her touch and talk and smile, and through her care. At an early age most of us learned from the women who looked after us, and from our first teachers who were women. My earliest memory is of being pushed through the lanes of the Welsh countryside by my mother and grandmother, of being exuberant at the colour and loveliness of the flowers and grass and wild-life along the roadside, and of being taught the words 'flower', 'tree', 'bird', 'grass' as they patiently encouraged my naive enthusiasm for the world around me, delighting in my delight – endorsing it, expanding it. This process of learning from women continues through formal education and professional training at every level, and through social and personal relationships. Women not only bring us to birth, they bring meaning into the life they give us, they shape it for us. Yet men can so readily forget all this. In the secret places of the heart, some men are afraid to learn from women. There is a deafness inside men, an ignoring of women, and a deluded formation of male identity which has its roots in the fear of women's power and skills.

In the New Testament incorporation implies transformation. 'If anyone is in Christ,' says St Paul, 'there is a new creation; the old order has passed away, behold, the new has come' (II Corinthians 5.17). To be 'in Christ' is to be part of his body, which is the church, truly the community of women and men found free and accounted equal by God in Christ. It is a reconciled community which continues the divine ministry of reconciliation initiated by God in Christ's living and dying

and rising again. It is a community in which men and women
are to be reconciled, their relationships transformed. They are
to receive from one another, be accountable to one another,
respect one another, honour one another. So women and men
are to be transformed by one another in and through the
working of the grace of the Holy Spirit.

What is it in women that men fear ?

I recall participating in a Christian conference which was
made up largely of men, with women in a small minority. The
conference consisted of a series of groups and workshops
reflecting on core sessions, in the way that these events
generally are. It took place before the issue of the ordination of
women had been decided upon by the General Synod, and
feelings were running high amongst the participants –
amongst the men as well as the women present. It seemed to
me that nearly all the women at the conference believed that
they had a call to be priests; most of them were already working in full-time ministry in parishes, and some had been
deaconesses for many years. It seemed that in every group and
every workshop a debate about gender relations within the
Church of England and within Christianity generally would
crop up, centred on the issue of women's ordination. In some
of the sessions in which I took part it was women who introduced the subject, at other times it was men.

One discussion I remember in particular, because it left
everyone feeling disturbed. At times in this discussion some of
the men were being deliberately hurtful and provocative. At
other times there was nothing intentional or malicious in the
men's behaviour, and yet the exchange was heated and con-
frontational, and the women who were attempting to discuss
the issues became 'upset'. The men were trying to engage in
'rational argument' with their women colleagues, often insist-
ing on the 'objective' truth of received doctrine and dismissing
what the women had to say. Though engaging in conventional
theological dispute with their male colleagues, the women
were also talking from experience and out of pastoral

encounter with people in the parishes. They cited their 'feelings' about their vocation to ordained ministry as evidence of
a call, authoritative evidence of which the church should take
account. Yet the men were unable to accept this as a convinc-
ing argument. Indeed, it seemed that the men there were able
to accept very little at all of the women's way of argument and
discussion. It seemed that their main aim was to dismiss the
women, to shut them up, to bury their perspectives, insights
and contributions under a mountain of ancient authority.
Now I look back on that encounter I imagine that the women
were feeling great pain and frustration at this lack of communication. Perhaps that is why the women began to cry.

I was a very fresh deacon, new to ecclesiastical politics, and
I recall feeling very uncomfortable in this session, and wishing
that all these contentious issues in the church would just go
away. I recall feeling dismayed by what seemed to be the
deliberate hurtfulness of some of my male colleagues. As a
'new boy' I was not a little intimidated myself at their fast and
insistent arguments. I can recall feeling very junior and inept
and unable to participate in the only way I knew how, which
was in some way to beat the men at their own arguments.
Most of all I remember being uneasy with the tears. I was
ashamed that the argument seemed to have 'got out of hand',
and sorry that people had been hurt; but what I wanted more
than anything was for the women to stop their crying. There
seemed to be something almost indecent about the tears, a
kind of subterfuge violence in the crying. What I wanted was
not for the women to cease their argument or change their
opinions or stifle their sense of call – indeed, my own convic-
tions about the rightness of the ordination of women made me
want their position to be victorious; not just accepted by all,
but accepted as incontrovertible. I wanted argument and hurt
to go away. What I wanted was what I suspect most of the
men in the group wanted, which was for the crying women to
'get a grip', pull themselves together, not get so worked up, do
the crying elsewhere. Though I am ashamed of it now, I
remember agreeing with the man who said to me afterwards
that the women should learn to get on with the job like men

have to rather than dissolving into tears: 'After all,' he said, 'what if we all started crying?!'

'What if we all started crying?'

What if we had? What if all the male clergy at that conference had given up talking about the prescribed topics on their tight and definite agendas and had started expressing what was truly concerning them? What if the male clergy there who were gay or overworked or anxious about finance or personal animosities within the parish or marital problems or sexual inadequacies or utter boredom with the church, what if they had sat in their groups and refused to cordon off all those questions and struggles about their identity and about their struggles within the community of the church, but had let it all come pouring out of them like some of their women colleagues had – and with tears if tears seemed the way to do it? What if the male priests who were so anxious about what the ordination of women might mean for them had been able to say so, rather than always talking the voice of reason, of scripture and tradition and definitive truth? What if there had been a voice from inside for the men to use, the voice of fear or hatred or rage or sorrow? What if the men had been able to talk the language of tears?

I am very glad that my sister clergy no longer have to cry in meetings because they are somehow required by men to 'prove' that women may exercise a priestly ministry – though I fear that those days are not entirely over within the church of two 'integrities'. But I am glad that the issue of women's ordination has been rationally, democratically debated and agreed upon, and that in this way the spiritual and sacramental realities have been opened up in a new perspective and given fresh expression within the Church of England. I am also grateful that those women, in their frustration and their anger, showed me a way of being and behaving within the church by their crying which I had not understood before. Though I could not learn the lesson at the time, what those tears did was to dissolve the pretence that theology or ecclesiastical business can be done whilst our feelings are left outside, somehow irrelevant or unaffected, and that the arguments about 'truth' within the church are in some way above the issues of power and control.

Now I interpret those tears as a demonstration against the sheer weight of hierarchicalism that seems to weigh down on so many church meetings – particularly meetings of the clergy – the code of ranking according to role and status, to age, 'experience', or organizational know-how, which operates within the community of faith as it goes about its business. In my experience there is very often a protocol of competition among the clergy which ensures that some will be exalted over others, who are relegated. The youthful, the newcomer, the uninitiated, the unassertive, the unmarried, the childless, the theologically inarticulate or indefinite are likely to be pushed to the bottom of the pile. Within this protocol of domination, which might be named *patriarchy*, to express weakness or a sense of failure or the need for support, means ruin. I have experienced women ministers participating in this protocol, too, establishing a hierarchy of 'pastoral awareness', as if caring were a matter of capacity and ministerial miles on the clock. Whatever the criteria, it seems to me, some must be placed at the bottom so that others may know themselves on top, evading challenge, controlling expression and defining the limits of acceptability.

Is this, perhaps, why we men were angry with those women for crying? Did we fear in those women a trickle of tears which might become a flood, a torrent which might wash away a house built on sand? Was it because the tears of those women threatened the foundations of an invulnerable church and of her invulnerable ministers? Was it because the tears exposed male control, male stability, male professionalism as a conceit, an unsatisfying restriction, a fiction which we were being required by the exposure of our own feelings and prejudices to rewrite? Was it because we men knew that the salt water of tears is the kind of solution which can peel away protective disguises, revealing our rage, leaving us with our pain exposed to ourselves and to others? Can it be that the tears threatened us with the loss of our power, and with possibilities too different and too free for us to contemplate? Could it be that, as on the first morning when the message of the women, of the outsiders – the message that he is risen – was too preposterous and terrifying to be believed in by the fear-filled men, so the message of those tears – the message of a free and strange future for the church – was too disturbing for us to accept? Had we become the outraged guests unable to interpret the beautiful thing done by the woman who had come in from outside?

Who is the outsider ?

Leo Tolstoy's tale 'Father Sergius' tells the story of a man whose self-understanding is changed by a woman whom he despised and regarded as valueless. The story begins in the imperial court of Russia. In the imperial guard there is a dashing young officer named Stephan Kasatsky. He is ambitious, talented and handsome. Kasatsky excels as a soldier and is a favourite of the Tsar, to whom Kasatsky is wholly devoted. Eager to achieve social success, Kasatsky courts a rich countess, the beautiful Mary Korotkova. Kasatsky worships her as a goddess, setting her on the pedestal of his adoration. Yet Kasatsky does not fully know the object of his desire. On the eve of their wedding day Mary confesses to him that she was once the mistress of the Tsar. Kasatsky is appalled. He breaks off their engagement, resigns his commission and enters a monastery in furious anger and bitter humiliation.

Within the confines of the monastery Kasatsky takes the name Sergius and quickly excels in the religious life, as he has done in all things previously. He is scrupulous in avoiding all worldliness and distraction. His severity of life marks him out from his brother monks. Yet when ecclesiastical ambition and the prospect of preferment threaten to hamper his pursuit of spiritual excellence, Father Sergius leaves the abbey to become a hermit. Living in a cave by the tomb of a saint, Sergius practises an austere asceticism, wary of demons and bodily temptations. His spiritual athleticism is heroic. In the middle of one freezing night an 'attractive divorcee', Madam Makovkina, comes to his cave pretending that she is lost, in an attempt to seduce Sergius. In vigorous patristic mode the hermit chops off one of his fingers in an effort to subdue the flesh and keep himself undefiled. His holiness becomes famed throughout all Russia. People flock to him for healing and spiritual guidance. Father Sergius becomes a focus for pilgrimage, a religious celebrity – and though inundated with people, he remains radically cut off from those who come to him.

Yet Sergius has not conquered those sexual desires he has battled so long to subdue. Secretly he sleeps with 'a devil', the sickly daughter of a merchant who is brought to him for healing. In despair at his failure Sergius feels compelled to take on yet another way of life, to pursue a deeper reality. He dreams of Pashenka, a girl he teased and bullied as a boy, whom he had despised as an 'insipid, insignificant, pathetic' woman, the ruined victim of a violent and drunken husband. Pashenka comes to represent a means of salvation for Sergius, and he sets out on pilgrimage to find the woman he once pitied and mocked. Penniless, he comes to Pashenka's house. She does not recognize the beggar at her door as Kasatsky, the proud young man she knew long ago, yet Pashenka welcomes the ragged man into her poor home and gives him money and food which she can ill afford.

Watching Pashenka's genuine humility and simple godliness, Sergius recognizes her as an authentic servant of Christ. Her sincerity exposes his self-deception: 'Pashenka is all that I should have been and was not. I lived for people, pretending it was for God, while she lives for God and thinks she is living for people.' Inspired by Pashenka's way of life, Father Sergius begins to let go of the identity he has built around his need for power and attainment. He begins to enjoy a new kind of holiness: 'The less he cared for the opinion of men, the more he felt the presence of God.' He calls himself simply 'a servant of God', and as a nameless vagrant he is exiled by the authorities

to Siberia, where he lives a life of simplicity and service as the
gardener of an affluent peasant.

Tolstoy's story is the story of a man learning from a woman.
At a moment of crisis Sergius remembers her; he begins to
listen to her life as it has spoken deep within his memory and
consciousness. Sergius, a powerful man, one who has pursued
and apparently achieved absolute success in career, morality
and religion, finds meaning and authenticity in a woman who
is not respected, a woman who is poor and marginal, a woman
whom he has ignored until he begins to hear the voices within himself, the voices of dissatisfaction, longing and weakness,
and then he can hear Pashenka's way of being, her challenge
to his continual striving, to the perfectionism which has
broken him. Pashenka's genuine and practical charity is an
epiphany, a showing forth of divine glory in the gloom of
Sergius' collapsed world. For though Pashenka is neither pure
virgin nor holy mother figure, the female types Sergius might
once have adored from afar and striven to emulate, yet in the
ordinariness of her living she is a Christ figure to the man who
once despised her. Sergius finds in her a new way, a freedom,
a mutuality. Father Sergius, the perfect priest, the holy man
who seems to the world to have achieved salvation, when he
listens to the voice of Pashenka's way of life, finds that she is
teaching him true holiness.

As Virginia Woolf wandered through Cambridge before
giving her talks to the women scholars of Girton and
Newnham, she may have passed St Bene't's Church. Despite
her status and power – or perhaps because of these things –
Woolf sees herself as an outsider in the academical world
which is the preserve of men. In the world of writing, all
women are outsiders. Woolf imagines the power of the outsider to challenge and transform. She imagines the Outsider,
the Woman Writer, member of the Society of Outsiders, walking her way round the colleges of her imaginary Oxbridge, an
unwelcome guest in a city which privileges men. Though we
do not know it, for Woolf does not say, this Woman Writer
might pass a church very like St Bene't's, and she might enter
it and see above the altar a window which depicts the figure

of a woman. She is a Pre-Raphaelite beauty – athletic, strong. Her hair is red and plentiful, falling about her shoulders in exuberant curls. Her lips are full, her jaw definite, her skin is pale, her eyes alive and full of light. The woman is kneeling on the ground and in her hands she has the feet of Jesus. She is resting his foot in her lap and surrounding it with her hair, and as she holds his feet she does not look up at him but looks away, somewhere beyond the present. Perhaps the woman looks toward the distant city, to Jerusalem and Calvary. And as she looks, let us suppose that she is drawing the Woman Writer toward herself, towards her encounter with the one whose flesh she holds and caresses. She draws all who see her towards the touching and the prophecy which is told in memory of her. And those who see this glass must wonder at the look she has upon her face. I am uncertain whether her look is one of invitation or challenge. Perhaps what the woman invites is challenge, both the prophetic woman of glass and the Woman Writer who watches her. And seeing them both in my mind's eye, as a man, I begin to understand that I do not understand – that there is another way which I must learn.

2

On Not Knowing What to Say

> One of the costs of the patriarchal practice of taking the male
> experience as normative for human experience is that men
> have become invisible to themselves. We rarely measure the
> measuring stick itself. But now that male conciousness is
> dawning ...   (James B. Nelson)[1]

I am writing this in my study. I am in my own private room, a
room in Cambridge. I have time and means with which to
write. The room is full of books, full of writing. Each volume
is a voice, a multiplicity of voices. I am sitting in a parliament
of voices, and like most parliaments, the voices I can hear are
the voices of men. Of course it is understood that women
speak and have always spoken: Sarah the matriarch; Esther
the queen; Deborah the judge; Ruth amidst the alien corn;
Hildegard the abbess, theologian, composer, poet; Mother
Julian the mystic; Teresa the confidante of popes and doctor of
the church; women poets, novelists, social reformers, theorists,
theologians, scientists, critics. But mainly it is men speaking in
these books, and there are so many of them, and they are so
learned, ancient, clever, wise, and their voices are so persis-
tent, and they speak so loudly, and with such confidence.

It is a wonder that any man dare say another word – least of
all about himself and other men – when men have done so
much talking already. It is a wonder that any man dare to say
another word when there are so many voices he must take into
account, who have said so much before he speaks, and who
have so much to say in answer when he has spoken.

The great tradition of men's voices is a strength, an invitation and encouragement for men to speak. Perhaps it may also
be a burden, an inhibition, a constraint for men. The vast

chorus of men raising their voices through the centuries with so much assurance and skill does not necessarily make it an easy thing for every man to speak.

The words of men and the Word of God

Imagine in your mind's eye the West façade of a Gothic cathedral – it might be Chartres or Wells; imagine yourself gazing up at the ranks of holy figures carved exquisitely in stone, a heavenly company set in niches mounting up to the skies. There they stand awaiting you in welcome and in judgment – mostly men: prophets, priests and kings, saints and martyrs, bishops, teachers, writers and evangelists. Imagine a façade of holy figures who are almost entirely male, towering above, holding their books, their swords, their croziers, their pens and keys and thuribles, bearded, bemitred, crowned and triple crowned, wholly celebrated and exalted here in their immaculate robes and vestments of chiselled stone. These are the patriarchs, the ancient and authoritative fathers of the faith. These are The Voices.

Amongst them can you see the prophet Jeremiah? Can you make him out, high up to the left, above the apostles, in an orderly row of Old Testament figures, all beards and straggling hair? How serene he is in the architectural grandeur, how severe and competent, a venerable man made wise by hardship, as if his struggles to speak and to be heard had lithified into an impenetrable rock over thousands of years. Jeremiah the prophet, set in stone, far from human reach, now untroubled by the world below, bearing his costly words inscribed between the covers of an enormous book carved so majestically from the rock, his volume of prophecies modelled with clasps, made safe in the securest of bindings by the church which reveres his utterances as holy.

Indeed Jeremiah the prophet *is* holy and worthy of veneration. But looking up at him here in this solid rank of the sanctified, who would remember the nature of his holiness, seeing him as he is represented now – invulnerable and accomplished in stone? Who would remember Jeremiah's anxiety, inadequacy and fear? Who could tell, now that they are spoken, recorded, revised, edited, enhanced by the community of the faithful, who could tell from looking at him there what those massive words cost him?

> Now the word of the Lord came to me saying,
> 'Before I formed you in the womb I knew you,
> and before you were born I consecrated you;
> I appointed you a prophet to the nations.'

> Then I said, 'Ah, Lord God! Behold,
> I do not know how to speak, for I am only a youth'
> (Jeremiah 1.4–6).

Jeremiah is a prophet: he is called by God to speak and given life; his life's mission is to speak the prophetic word, and yet he is afraid. On his part there is a profound sense of unworthiness, the sense of inability to fulfil this divine commission: a proper prophetic humility in the one who is the human mouthpiece for the divine message. We forget too easily, perhaps, that this ancient authority, this prophet of Israel through whom the Holy Spirit spoke and still speaks, found his speaking difficult. The account of the commissioning of Jeremiah incorporates the memory of a deep unease in Jeremiah because he is young: *'I do not know how to speak, for I am only a youth.'* Jeremiah feels himself to be unqualified, inadequate, knowing nothing, lacking in seniority and appropriate status. He does not know *how* to speak. He has nothing of the artifice or skill, the self-conception or confidence, the internal authority, to speak as he has experienced speaking being done: Jeremiah feels unable to speak as a man should speak. Being a youth he has no place in the hierarchy of those who do the speaking, he has no natural or social platform, he is unable to speak from a position of power in the face of power. All the authoritative words of the priests and the prophets and the powerful of Jerusalem are not an encouragement to Jeremiah; the vast social, theological, ideological language of male talk is not one in which he has the means to participate. Though a man, he has no place; he feels he has no voice to *compete* with the voices of other men.

The voice with which God calls the prophet to speak is one which bears a message different from those other familiar voices, of which he is afraid.

> But the Lord said to me,
> 'Do not say, "I am only a youth";
> for to all to whom I send you you shall go,
> and whatever I command you you shall speak.
> Do not be afraid of them,
> for I am with you to deliver you, says the Lord.'
> Then the Lord put forth his hand and touched my mouth;
> and the Lord said to me,
> 'Behold, I have put my words in your mouth' (1. 7–9).

The voice which Jeremiah shall speak is not a voice to join the chorus of established voices. He is to voice God's word, a voice given to him, a calling to speak of that which is beyond himself and yet deep within himself, a voice given when he was in the womb. Jeremiah finds a voice which was given in his time of total weakness and defencelessness, a powerful voice which is rooted in the time when he was wholly dependent upon his mother, entirely reliant upon her nourishment and strength. It is a voice given in the time which is out of time, the womb-time of being, receiving, growing without striving or achievement or qualification. The prophetic voice is one which has no authority except that of God, a voice which by its graciousness, its givenness, sets the prophet against the voices of patriarchal tradition which speak in their own strength and for their own gain. The voice of the prophet offers a critique of that which is taken for the norm, a voice arising outside convention to challenge it, the voice 'crying in the wilderness', the voice of one who remembers his time in the womb, who knows that his life is at its source one of relation, of being nurtured by another, sustained even now by others. His voice is to speak a language of connection, interdependence, and truth. Jeremiah's speaking is to expose all

talk which is insincere or corrupt ('Do not trust in these decep-
tive words:"This is the temple of the Lord, the temple of the
Lord"', 7.4), the prophet and priest who speak with popular
authority the inauthentic *word* ('saying "Peace, peace" when
there is no peace', 6.14), who claim to speak on God's behalf
and yet no longer listen to God's word, which is the voice of
justice and true faithfulness:

> Their tongue is a deadly arrow; it speaks deceitfully;
> With his mouth each one speaks peaceably
> with his neighbour,
> but in his heart he plans an ambush (9.8).

The words of the priest and the prophet are words of
exploitation, they speak a language of violence and disposses-
sion. Their talking has been severed from all connection with
the heart, it does not arise out of listening to the longing of
God for his people, or from the conscience, or from the
promptings of pity and compassion: it is disobedient talk,
garrulous self-interest, a weaponry of words for conspiracy
and assault against all those who speak another voice, voices
which challenge their power:

> Come let us make plots against Jeremiah, for the law shall
> not perish from the priest, nor from the council of the wise,
> nor from the word of the prophet. Come let us smite him
> with the tongue, and let us not heed any of his words
> (18.18).

The prophet suffers for what he has to say; to speak the
word of justice brings punishment and abuse: 'the word of the
Lord has become for me a reproach and derision all day long'
(20.8). Yet it is a voice of inner pleasure which he speaks, a
delicious language of discovery and the overflowing of spiritual nourishment: 'Thy words were found, and I ate them, and
thy words became to me a joy and the delight of my heart; for
I am called by thy name' (15.16). Jeremiah's experience is of a
God who gives the outsider voice. God's voice is not like the
voices of violence and false promises, not like the voices of

which Jeremiah is afraid, the voices of the men of power who speak so loudly and convincingly the certainties which marginalize and silence and are a denial of the truth. God's voice is the voice of encouragement: *'Do not be afraid'*. God's voice is not a voice in union with the voices of the powerful talkers. It speaks differently, challenging the pretences of a monolithic culture which denies variety and is deaf to the multiplicity of voices. God's voice is the voice which draws out other voices, a gifting voice, a subversive voice, a word against all talk which seeks to drown out the voices of the poor, of those who feel themselves to be voiceless – even in their own relationships and in their own hearts. It calls out to the silenced to singspeak their stories, to find a voice which is an authentic voice amid the lying voices of injustice and self-deceit, the soothing voices of corrupted religion, the competing voices of vying male authority.

The struggle for men to speak without shouting

Jeremiah has not been carved alone in that façade. He is there with a myriad of men. The men are silent. The men are stone. The men are dead. These men are the Voices. We may see the men as glowering down on us in fury and resentment. We may see the men as angry, as speechless, as spent. The men are feeling nothing, saying nothing, doing nothing but keeping up their postures and positions in their hierarchy of rock. These are petrified men, men keeping up a front. These men are preserving a façade. These men have been constructed into a wall of frigid silence in which they stand without touching or talking, separated from one another, looking outward, looking ahead, determined to let nothing by, to let nothing out. In the mutuality of their isolation these men have formed a mask, a barricade, a dam.

So, once more, who are these men of stone lined up before us? Peter is there, chief of the apostles, Vicar of Christ, Bishop of Rome. Peter who holds the keys to heaven and hell, who may bind and loose, who is strong enough to strengthen his brethren in their faith. There he is, resolute, eternal, authoritative, in charge: 'You are Peter, and on this rock I will build my church.' Beside him Paul, apostle to the Gentiles, urgent preacher, indefatigable traveller, irrepressible evangelist, teacher, pastor, missionary; Paul who is constantly addressing, admonishing, encouraging the faithful; visiting them, writing to them, making appeals to their purses and their consciences. Paul the tireless labourer, sowing the seeds of the gospel, building the church, always working to pay his own way and never giving up.

Above these two mighty apostles are the patriarchs: Moses the powerful liberator, the compelling leader, the scourge of Pharaoh, who led his people like sheep, divided the sea, found a way through the desert, kept his community together through forty years of travelling and turmoil; Moses who climbed the holy mountain and stood on holy ground, who talked with God and entered into the divine presence, whose face shone with the glory of the divine being. With Moses are the prophets, Jeremiah's many brothers, from Amos to Zephaniah – the whole company who utter God's word, channels for that active power which cannot return to him fruitless; full of insight, anger, denunciation, promise. And mingled among them are kings and judges – the warrior David: dancer, lover, conqueror, founder of a wonderful kingdom and winner of a splendid empire.

And further above, almost with the angels, the fathers of the churches, the deciders and protectors of orthodoxy, the teachers and expositors of truth, the formulators of orthopraxis and explicators of belief, the venerable chroniclers of the church: there they are too, with their books and cardinal's hats – Bede, the Gregorys, Athanasius, Aquinas. Among them is Augustine, astonishing intelligence and seeker after truth, who standing up there with a crowd of episcopal dunces makes them wise by association. There they all are towering above us, men of stone.

These fine statues might be for us memorials which deny the fleshliness of men, the flawedness and ineptitude of men. These heroes may have been carved and assembled to promote the patriarchal constructions of masculine autarchy and omnicompetence. We might see in all this soaring triumpha- lism a concealment of oppressive practice, a deafness to the voices of the poor, an exclusion of those not represented – that is, the suppression of women.

And, it is true, women are excluded from this pantheon of heroic virtue, except for half a dozen virgins and queens, and Mary the virgin mother: women whose sexuality has been subdued or quietly laid aside. Why seek to deny it? This façade is a men-fest, a celebration of men selected by men for a church dominated by men – a culture in which women have been placed on the margins. Some of the texts which these figures hold and the ideas and values which they represent are shot through with a hatred and a fear and an ignorance of women. And not only women, but homosexuals also. Here is a tradition which has been formed in the denial, denigration and destruction of those who speak a voice which differs from the Voices of the powerful.[2]

May we take another view, look again, see differently?

Perhaps these men placed there in that solid majesty are prisoners in stone. They are prisoners of the way in which their words and actions have been interpreted. These men have been cast in a mode which is alien to them, victims of a conspiracy in stone to subdue their fallible flesh, their pound- ing hearts, their faltering, stuttering words. Perhaps these Voices are exhibits in an architectural charade, a diversion from that which is uncomfortable and costly in the process of speaking and writing and witnessing to truth. Have these men been assembled as they are – presented as invulnerable, incon- trovertible – to give the lie to their struggle and pain in gain- ing understanding and finding expression? Perhaps all this celebration of accomplished volumes and spoken sermons and accepted teachings is an avoidance of men's wrestling with their inability to speak, their battle to communicate honestly, to say what is truly the case, to make authentic expression. Perhaps this tower of men is a monumental denial of impotence, a terrifying parade of talkers, writers, builders, teachers, founders, reformers, of doers and sayers – a carnival of eloquence – which is all distraction from the tiny, agonizing

pain of inarticulacy, from the risk of vulnerability, an evasion
of men's dreadful fear of failure.

For what we might see here are men of stone who have been
carved in celebration of God's gift of a heart of flesh. Perhaps
these men may represent the workings of divine power
among a people who have no power or eloquence, the calling
together of the marginal and voiceless, the transformation of
self-interest, violence and abuse into the voices of repentance,
justice and love.

For in looking at these stone men we might see them less as
a demand for competency and adequacy from those always
above and beyond us, but more as a sculpture of grace, a form
given to creation out of nothing, more as a memorial dedi-
cated to the miraculous finding of a voice. For who is the Rock,
this great stone man, but *Peter* – the man of flesh, the man of
failure, the man of so much wasted and misplaced effort? Who
is his partner there but *Saul of Tarsus*, the persecutor, the man
so full of assurance and religious zeal who was so sorely and
viciously misguided; who, once he has been granted light to
see, becoming the apostle, no longer lives out of his successes,
which become to him as rubbish, but always thereafter out of
his failures, rejections and inabilities gathered up and put to
new work by God's grace in Christ. Above them is Moses, the
great leader who demanded liberty from the hard-hearted
Pharaoh though he had begged God not to send him but to
send some other, who cannot believe God's power to give him
voice to speak to the powerful and to those deafened by
oppression: 'But behold, they will not believe me or listen to
my voice, for they will say "The Lord did not appear to you"'';
Moses who was dumb with the sense of his own inadequacy
and ineptitude: 'Oh my Lord, I am not eloquent, either hereto-
fore or since thou hast spoken to thy servant; but I am slow of
speech and of tongue' (Exodus 4.10). With him are Samuel,
chosen as a boy in the temple, and David, the least among his
brothers, the youth barely thought of, who was anointed as
God's chosen one. Isaiah is there, the man who pleaded with
God to depart from him because he was unworthy to receive
God's commission, a man afraid of the voice which might sear

his lips because he was a man from among a people of unclean lips. It is not only women who have been terrified by the Voices, shouted into silence by their grandeur and faultlessness. It is not only children, black people, gay people, the young, the dependent old, not only those who have wished to speak another language of justice or complaint. Men, too, are silenced when they see these bigger, better, cleverer, louder Voices. Men have tried to find a niche for themselves, a hiding-place in the great façade. Men have sought to become stone; to be the Patriarch, the Father, to speak as a Voice, *the* Voice which knows no ambiguity or diversity from which to speak. To be stone has seemed far safer, proper, more powerful. To be stone has seemed incontrovertible, unaccountable, impenetrable. To be stone is not to have to climb down from the pedestal and be flesh.

But if men were able to see these men of stone as less of an impossible target to match, less of an unmeetable challenge to our own faltering expressions, less a constraint or an obligation, and more of an invitation to authenticity, then men should see these figures as an encouragement in finding a voice, a multiplicity of voices. If men listen to these Voices, they will hear the memories of failure and of grace, the expression of human weakness, inarticulacy, error, inadequacy – a lament which is the starting point of new life and understanding.There is a voice amongst the Voices, the *still small voice* whispering to us of a voice for ourselves, voices from deep within ourselves, the voice of voices which are honest, just, repentant, responsive, sustainable: a gift.

A new heart I will give you, and a new spirit I will put within you; and I will remove from your body the heart of stone and give you a heart of flesh. I will put my spirit within you … and you shall be my people, and I will be your God (Ezekiel 36.26–27).

The Gospels as memories of failure and narratives of grace

Among the works in the Galleria dell'Accademia in Florence
is Michelangelo's marble sculpture 'Awakening Slave'. The
sculpture is among his unfinished works, and so the shape of
a man emerges from the rock half-formed, as if a human life is
awakening out of dead stone, struggling to break free and
have existence, movement, sensation, relationship. The man is
naked, stretching, rising out of sleep with face and limbs and
genitals straining to have expression and pulse, but as yet
indefinite. Michelangelo worked with an aesthetic theory of
sculptural subtraction in which the artist, chiselling his rock,
lets the imprisoned idea-form be liberated into being: 'by
taking away ... one puts/ into hard and alpine stone/ a figure
that's alive/ and that grows larger wherever the stone
decreases ... '[3] So the dead stone falls away to unfold living
flesh, a slow and careful process of emergence. The unfinished
'Awakening Slave' articulates all this. Some of the books of the
New Testament allude to this same sense of process, of awakening – the falling away of blindness and incomprehension,
the emergence of a community of belief, the dawning of
understanding for individuals. St Paul writes of this explicitly
in his images of the new life in Christ and the process of
sanctification, maturing, and deepening of knowledge which
is involved for personality and church as the old ways are
put off and the new are assumed (e.g. Ephesians 4.11ff.; II
Corinthians 5.15ff., Colossians 1.28ff.). The Gospels, too, are
full of this movement from misunderstanding to comprehen-
sion, disbelief to faith, fear to trust, denial and desertion to
discipleship and mission. In particular the resurrection
experiences seem to be about a dawning of the truth of God's
work in Christ amongst those who have followed him. Not
even the resurrection is a matter of instant understanding or
total belief, but a process of awakening among the disciples.

   In the Gospel of St Mark this movement is sculpted in the
emergent text: initially the Gospel ended with the discovering
by the Marys and Salome of the fearful truth of the empty
tomb, which must be kept as a strange and dangerous secret

(16.8). Then later the experience of Jesus' presence by Mary Magdalene and others is added to the original text of the author, and this experience is not believed until the apostles themselves have sight of him, a faith in his resurrected life which finds expression in the risen Christ's command to go into all the world (16.15), and the disciples' movement outwards into all places comes as Christ assumes all power at the right hand of God. This is a movement from terror and secrecy, through unbelief, to proclamation and service.

In the final chapter of St Luke's Gospel, the two travellers walking to Emmaus are slow to understand the meaning of Christ's death and blind to the risen Lord: God's purposes dawn on them as the stranger who journeys with them unfolds the message of the scriptures, and in the breaking of the bread they recognize Christ – 'their eyes were opened' – the Unfolder unfolded. Even as the risen Christ appears to his disciples, some doubt (Matthew 28.17; Luke 24.41; John 20.24ff.), most are terrified (Matthew 28.10; Luke 24.37; John 20.19); the resurrection joy is mingled with fear and incredulity and a sluggishness of understanding. So in Acts the Spirit is given to a confused, troubled, uncertain group of people who have glimpsed something more wonderful than they are able, yet, fully to understand. Peter proclaims the death of Christ (Acts 2.14ff.) without yet having grasped its full implications for himself and for the Jewish nation in relation to the Gentiles – an understanding which comes later, in his encounter with Cornelius (Acts 10). In John, Christ comes with a greeting of peace to people who are, as yet, uncertain of him; he breathes the Holy Spirit upon a group who meet in secrecy and fear, disappointment and grief. It is in the midst of all the swirling exuberance and poverty of human understanding and emotional response that the risen Christ is known or not known, and it is in all the chaos of human personality and community that his resurrection takes root and grows.

It is time perhaps for men to recover the Gospels as memories of failure, as stories of flesh rather than authorities set in stone. In the midst of failure the church first knew the resurrection of Christ, and in the light of that rising learnt to value the stories of failure as narratives of grace. The Gospels do not witness to the successes of those who sought to follow Jesus of Nazareth, but to their foolishness, pride, stubbornness, misapprehension, weakness, fear. For the Peter who confesses Jesus as the Christ, Cephas – Peter the Rock – is he who immediately tries to dissuade Christ from his sacrificial death (Mark), who argues with him at the washing of the feet (John), the one who tries to resist Jesus' arrest (Luke), who abandons him, denies him, disbelieves the women who have seen him risen from the dead (John). And surely the memories of Peter's failings are representative communally as well as personally, stories which carry the burden of the others' failings – communal memories of the lack of trust, understanding, loyalty and strength which were the failings of the other disciples also, and the failings of disciples ever since.

We have the memories of Judas betraying his leader, Thomas doubting and Mary mistaking him for a gardener; memories of his family questioning his sanity, his disciples scrabbling for precedence and repeatedly misinterpreting his identity, teaching and mission. They excluded the children from him, were perplexed at his demands of them, fell asleep in their last moments with him, and finally fled at his arrest and abandoned him to his trial and execution. Woven into the narratives which unfold the identity and work of Jesus is all the reluctance, dimness and misunderstanding of those who followed him, as well as the explicit lack of faith of those who did not believe and openly rejected him. That Christ's ministry was given and continued in and through the failures as well as the faith of his followers is integral to the good news.

At the close of the Gospel of John, which tells of the beloved disciple who stayed with his friend at the cross, all these failures are gathered up and given a new meaning in the restoration of Peter. The disciple who denied his Lord three times is three times given by the risen Christ the opportunity to speak of his love for him. In love, the voice of Christ draws out from Peter his expression of love – not of sorrow, not of guilt, apology or regret, but only of love. As he does so, Christ commands Peter to nourish those who seek to follow in the way and to give his own life in discipleship and witness. Peter is chosen not for his perfection but because he is healed. In a sense, he is an apostle because of his flaws – and it is out of his weaknesses and failures that he must lead, by grace.

For the voice of which John's Gospel speaks, the voice which will strengthen those who seek to follow Christ, the voice which will come alongside them and remind them of all that he has said, the voice which will teach them all the truth, the voice which Peter is given – the voice of the Holy Spirit – is the voice which draws others to speak, which makes quiet within, which makes a community of voices quiet, so that others may be heard, so that the conscience may speak, so that God may find a voice. The voice of the Holy Spirit recounts the memories of failure within the story of forgiveness so that the new beginnings may be spoken of, the Spirit breathing on dry bones so that they may live.

Finding a voice

Men who do not know what to say for themselves may find a voice in response to a gospel which articulates failure and incorporates failure. A voice which speaks the memories of failure could encourage men to cease in the attempts to be the faultless, omniscient, omnicompetent Voice, and to find a voice for themselves, an authentic voice, one which arises from the realities of men's experience.

It is, of course, absurd on one level to suggest that men are without a voice. The voices of television, radio, papers, books, art, culture, academia, industry, religion, economics, in military might and personal, sexual relations; for the most part across the world the dominant voices of opinion and policy – the Voices of power – are those of men. But at the same time these Voices terrify men into silence because they wish to speak only the language of power and not any other language, least of all the language of repentance.

3

Men's Voices

We are now in a situation where there is a historical opportunity to look at the role of men – in their relationship to
women, to one another and to society.   (David Cohen)[1]

The aim of this chapter is to describe the cultural and social
theatre in which men are currently rehearsing theories and
feelings about themselves as men. This is a prelude to the
following chapters, which undertake to give a brief survey
of some examples of current attempts at expressing men's
self-understanding. In particular, the 'Men's Movement'
characterized by the work of Robert Bly and his book *Iron John*,
the 'Constructionist' theorization of men and masculinity, and
then Christian attempts to remodel maleness on the masculinity of Jesus Christ.

Learning to talk

In an earlier chapter is an exploration of the story in the
Gospels of the woman who anoints Jesus. The different
versions of the story offer us powerful images of the strength
of women who are excluded from the community: the
strength of the woman who weeps in the acknowledgment
of her need, and the power of the woman who makes her
prophecy from the margins. In both versions of the story the
women are outsiders, intruders, and their actions are met with
the indignation and disapproval of the men present, who mis-
interpret their meaning. Yet what the women are embracing
through their open expression of need and love (Luke) and
through the public proclamation of a difficult truth (Mark) is a
gospel which is for all people, and especially for those who are

discounted in the conventional way of things. The women witness to the reality that in Christ, God has put down the mighty from their seat and exalted the humble and meek. The women proclaim and demonstrate a gospel of transformed relationships, of transformed being. Theirs is a gospel which implies change in power relations, and from the perspective of a world now influenced by the ideas and practice of feminism, a gospel which implies a change in the relations of women and men. In those Gospel stories the expectations and perceptions of the male disciples and the men of religion are displaced by the intruding woman, who proclaims a different gospel, one which challenges and subverts the theologies and religious practices of her outraged brothers. Imagine the dismay, fury and humiliation of Simon the Leper and of the disciples as the realities of Jesus dawn on them. What the story of the woman anointing Jesus implies is a moment of massive re-assessment for the men who stood by and witnessed her actions – actions which she did *for herself* and not as some kind of show for the men.

Feminist scholars such as Elisabeth Schüssler Fiorenza have reinterpreted the story of the woman anointing Christ as part of a recovery of a hidden tradition within the Christian community of women being fully integrated and participative at all levels of life in that community. These reinterpretations have not been undertaken primarily in order to convince men of women's integral place within Christian belief, thought and practice; feminist theology has been done by women for women. But clearly there are implications arising out of this enterprise for men. Transformation in the self-understanding of women implies transformation for men. A debate has arisen within the Christian churches (albeit somewhat reluctantly) about the place of women within them, and increasingly there is a movement away from addressing 'women's issues' in isolation, as if women were intruding upon what is essentially male ecclesiastical ground, towards an exploration of the relations between women and men in the church – an opening out of the debate towards questions of gender relations. As part of this, men have begun to explore their own self-

understanding *vis-à-vis* women and their relationships with
one another.[2]

Men have begun to write and talk about themselves *as men*.
There is nothing new in men talking and writing about their
own concerns. What is specific to the attention men are now
paying to themselves is that it has developed in response to
the women's movement, initiated particularly by the feminism of the 1960s and 1970s. Men have begun to develop a
process of writing and discussion which articulates a critical
awareness of the social roles and self-understanding of men in
the light of feminist thought and practice. The focus is on men
as men, on masculinity and male identity, in relation to
women as they are identifying themselves through the
women's movement and in the light of feminist ideas and consciousness. Change for women implies change for men – or
reaction against such change. This work has been called the
Men's Movement and also Men's Studies.

As feminism has changed the way in which men understand themselves in relation to women, it has brought about a
moment of crisis for men. Feminist politics has begun to
expose, challenge and change the power relations between
men and women in society. In the feminist analysis, the whole
social order is patriarchal: men have power over women in
every area of life – economic, social, intellectual, personal,
sexual. The women's movement in the modern era has been a
movement in which women have articulated their oppression
by men within this system, and, having identified this oppression, work for transformation towards an order of equality
and mutuality which embodies the common values women
have begun to experience and enjoy amongst themselves.

Given the operation of gender awareness in all spheres now,
undergirded by feminism, it is no longer feasible for men to
retain an 'innocence' about a culture which works in their
favour to the detriment of women. This is what Virginia Woolf
was able to demonstrate as she exposed the male exclusivity of
the British establishment. If women are kept outside by men,
if they are excluded by male institutions, then by their very
'outsideness' – once women identify this place of exclusion as

a place of power – they will begin to marginalize the establishment, exposing the absurdity and the injustice of its bias, showing that what seems 'natural' is constructed and devised for the purposes of control and privilege. Men can no longer assume that their experience is universal (that their voices are The Voices).

Within the churches, for example, there are massive implications for men as well as for women as the voices of women theologians and biblical scholars draw our attention to the male bias of theology and scholarship, and to the patriarchal nature of the sacred texts and institutions:

> The way in which Scripture has been read by women has opened up many perspectives lost to predominantly white male interpreters. The process of recovery of women's voices in the Christian tradition and the insights yielded from the text when looked at from women's points of view can shake our complacency about the irredeemably patriarchal character of Scripture and the tradition of the church.[3]

A range of questions affecting every aspect of the life and thought of the Christian community arises out of feminism: no longer can it be just an isolated matter of 'women's issues' within the church or in any other sphere of common life. This reassessment among men is widespread and multi-faceted. An early response to the women's movement of the 1960s and 1970s was that some men, albeit very few, began to articulate an 'anti-sexist' stance in solidarity with women, responding to the feminist analyses of sexual politics from their own perspective as men. The editorial of the first issue of *Achilles Heel*, a magazine established in 1978 as a forum for discussion about men and masculinity, articulated the sense that unequal power relations between the sexes distorted men as well as women:

> Our power in society as men not only oppresses women but imprisons us in a deadening masculinity which cripples all our relationships – with each other, with women, with ourselves.[4]

Feminism gave birth to a new search for self-understanding and expression in men which has continued and diversified. The women's movement created a shift in the relations between women and men in such a way that some men felt an imperative to articulate their feelings about themselves as men, somehow to give account of themselves, to answer accusations or explain situations, or to come to terms with how they saw themselves in the light of women's self-understanding and the analyses of patriarchy. The resulting literature suggests that many men who have encountered aspects of feminism have felt angry and afraid in varying degrees. Some have reacted to it with hostility, with verbal or physical violence. Some have felt aggrieved or misrepresented. Others have found it an opportunity and a liberation. What seems to be general amongst many men is a sense, whether spoken or concealed, that men are experiencing a crisis of identity.

The reflexive context and the problem of language

The sociologist Anthony Giddens has suggested that contemporary social life is a *reflexive society* in which all aspects of human activity are the subject of constant analysis and description, and, as a consequence of these processes, continuing change. In this context of reflexivity the whole complex make-up of personal identity as it is constituted in social relationship is under review and reinterpretation. In modern society every aspect of self has an 'open character'. Identity becomes like the centre of a large city, constantly being surveyed, developed and re-built :

> The self today is for everyone a reflexive project – a more or less continuous interrogation of past, present and future. It is a project carried on amidst a profusion of reflexive resources: therapy and self-help manuals of all kinds, television programmes and magazine articles.[5]

Human sexuality exemplifies this reflexive way of being. The work of Jacques Foucault shows that once sexuality is no longer bound up with human reproduction, through the availability of effective contraception, it becomes 'plastic', to be shaped by the desires and will of the individual, who is informed by the ongoing, shifting conversation on sexuality within society. Giddens suggests that this discourse on sexuality exemplifies the modern reflexive society as it not only describes human`sexual relations, but comes to constitute the social reality it portrays. So the medical study and clinical categorization of sexual acts between men which was under-taken in the nineteenth century led to the establishment of a homosexual identity.[6] By such reflexive analysis, sexual iden-tity becomes a component in the construction of self. Foucault suggests that sexuality has become the 'great sermon' of con-temporary living, part of the 'Californian cult of the self', in which the modern individual continually seeks to discover his or her 'true being', set free from all that hinders or obscures it.[7]

Men, masculinity, male identity and male sexuality – these have emerged as issues in a culture which is busy with the discovery of self and the design of personal identity. A range of literature and a plethora of debates, a discourse, has been spawned in the West as men consider themselves as men. Introducing a collection of essays on men, Jeff Hearn com-ments on the philosophy undergirding the book: ' ... men and masculinities are not seen as unproblematic, but as social con-structions which need to be explored, analysed, and indeed in certain respects ... changed'.[8] These words might also serve as a more general, social description.

This enterprise of masculine self-reflection is not under-taken in isolation from other social conversations. Current writing and thinking on masculinity is informed by other emerging consciousnesses such as those of race and sexual orientation as well as feminism, so that the term *masculinities* is often preferred in order to convey the awareness of variety and difference amongst men and in forms of masculine self-understanding.[9] The social sciences have provided tools for analysis, and psychological and sociological surveys offer data which can further notions of self-understanding among men.

But it is psychoanalytical theory which provides men with a language for the exploration, articulation and transformation of 'self':

> Psychoanalysis may not be true; it may not solve anything. But it has created a vocabulary in which we can discuss where our lives are and our options. It has affected the way in which we think of ourselves and how we imagine changing ourselves. For men, it makes it possible to think about the kinds of men we want to be.[10]

For Lynne Segal, a feminist commentator on men and masculinity, psychoanalytical theory offers the only means for understanding 'the measure of internal conflicts and fragile sexual identities which trouble and torment the minds of men'. For Anthony Easthope the shifting internal structures of self which psychoanalysis reveals make it a tool which demythologizes conventional masculinity whilst also offering a means for transformation.[11]

Yet the task of finding an appropriate language in which to speak of men and masculinity is also acknowledged as difficult and complicated. In his study of masculine subjectivity Peter Middleton qualifies his aim of creating 'an emancipatory men's discourse' with the suspicion that to look inward will require 'a constant checking of the very process of turning analysis back on the analyst'. The reflexive enterprise is intensely self-aware:

> No one can innocently use terms like 'men', 'representation', 'subjectivity', 'emancipatory', 'discourse' or 'emotion'. These are the cruxes of contemporary debate which signal not only intellectual disagreement but institutional, political and national differences.[12]

Middleton goes on in his book to offer a critique of psychoanalytical theory as it is applied in the theories of sexual difference. This loss of innocence in language and theory extends even to the notion of rationality itself. The sociologist Vic

Seidler suggests that the modes of reason employed by men within the dominant Cartesian philosophy compound men's lack of self-understanding, for these systems of thought are fragmentary, separating mind from body, and leaving no place for the integration of lived experience, emotion or the perspectives of personal identity in the formation of meaning and self-understanding. Bob Connell urges all study of masculinity to recognize that the clinical method of Freud, demonstrated in his case history of the 'Wolf Man', is unsurpassed in 'separating layer after layer of emotion and mapping the shifting relationships between them', and that 'no approach is adequate that has not absorbed this lesson about the tensions within masculine character and its vicissitudes through the course of a life'.[14] Yet psychoanalysis provides a diversity of knowledge which sustains conflicting analyses of masculinity, and which, when taken in isolation from the insights of other disciplines, negates the full reality of the physical and the social in men's lives. Arguing for the role of the social sciences in the study of masculinity, Connell sees (Freudian) psychoanalytical theory as an essential tool, the worth of which 'will depend upon our ability to grasp the structuring of personality and the complexities of desire at the same time as the structuring of social relations, with their contradictions and dynamisms'.[15]

Wendy Cope has written an amusing and trenchant poem called 'Men and their boring arguments'. Whilst the familiar scene of the poem is a pub where men have had one too many and become involved in a 'crucial' debate in which neither 'side' can bear to lose or allow anyone else to participate, the poem intends a more general criticism of the way in which men conduct their search for meaning: too much heat, very little light. Yet the production of theory in the masculinity debate – arguments about argument – is a recognition that if men are to express themselves with any meaning then the language and theory of these expressions must be authentic and appropriate. In the articulation of problems will lie the genesis of solutions. This is to recognize that self-understanding for men has personal and social effects. Some see these effects in

terms which are 'therapeutic' for the individual. Others understand them as political, propelling social and cultural change.
Most make links between the personal and the political, and,
emulating the collective approach of the women's movement,
find that men's groups are the place in which masculinity is
most perceptively, creatively and safely explored – in terms of
both the individual and of society. Much of what is written
about men by men has arisen out of these groups, just as the
corporate self-discovery of the women's movement was the
source of much feminist theory and agenda for change.

Men who are undertaking an exploration of masculinity at
the present time do so in the light of feminism and in the
context of a reflexive society in which masculine identity and
self-understanding will not be considered in isolation from
other awarenesses such as those of race, class and sexuality.
These explorations have been termed Men's Studies – a broad
term which does something to convey the variety of men's
thinking and writing about their identity and experience. This
reflection is multi-disciplinary in nature: psychological, sociological, anthropological, psychoanalytical and, more recently,
theological. It is characterized by an acute critical self-
awareness and by the primacy of personal experience articulated by an individual or by a convened group of men.

Masculinity or masculinities?

Two broad approaches towards men's self-understanding can
be identified within men's studies, which might be termed
essentialism and *constructionism*. For essentialists, manhood
may be located in an essential masculinity which is 'within' all
men, from which men have become dislocated and with which
they must be reunited. An inner healing is to be made
available to men which finds expression in the work of the
mythopoeic writings of Jungian analysts and commentators.
In contrast, the constructionist approach is informed by the
social sciences, and understands 'masculinity' as a construction of social forces, the product of culture, always defined in
relation to that which is 'feminine'. Conventional masculini-

ties are understood as an outworking of men's power over women under patriarchy. In this understanding the healed man will be a reconstructed man, the bearer of a socially reconstructed masculinity.

Though these two approaches are contrasting and may be in opposition, often versions of each may be found operating together in parts of the men's movement. Men are being influenced by both strands toward change. Both approaches have contributed to the developing theology of men who are participating in the self-reflexive enterprise within the Christian community – a theology which is as diverse and inter-connected as the range of men's studies, with similar emphases and weaknesses. The essentialist approach can be characterized as individualist, yet it draws on Jung's powerful sense of the collective and often encompasses a social dimension. The constructionist approach has a societal emphasis which has strong personal implications. Both recognize that the personal and the social are integrally bound up, and yet both are criticized as evading the reality of men's oppression of women in varying degrees. In both there is a search for feeling and expression, an attempt to find a voice which breaks 'the silence of an undeveloped or lost language' among men.[16]

Men and masculinity: theory and practice

It would be wrong, however, to suggest that the whole enterprise of men's reassessment of their identity and role is literary and confined to the academic sphere. Indeed, most of the literature and thinking which constitutes men's studies arises out of a wider, diverse movement which undertakes 'men's work': that is, individuals or groups of men who undertake to reflect upon men and masculinity in a formal therapeutic context or in less structured settings. This may involve a man exploring his identity and functioning as a man with a therapist who specializes in attending to issues of masculinity, or it may be a matter of belonging to a men's group. Some of these groups are facilitated and guided by men who have particular emphases in philosophy and

approach to men's issues – such as the mythopoeic approach
characterized by Robert Bly and James Hillman, or by a more
political anti-sexist stance. In general, different ideas flow into,
and out of, one another, and stimulate a variety of understanding and analysis. The ways in which men are exploring
their identities and roles are as multifarious as there are means
within the reflexive society.

Furthermore, professionals within areas of health, education, social work, crime/probation and human resources/per-
sonnel work are beginning to pay specific attention to men
and men's issues. For example, some organizations are now
focussing on issues of men's health within their occupational
health strategies, recognizing that statistically men are particularly vulnerable to specific diseases and that they are less
likely to seek medical help than women. Advice on patterns of
work and stress management, diet, sexual practice and a range
of health issues are being tailored to address men within
preventative health strategies. This is also the case where professionals are responding to men's involvement in crime. In
some probation departments and prisons men convicted for
committing violent crimes against women participate in
group work which aims to confront, examine and reform their
behaviour as men.

Literature about men and masculinity grows out of and
refers back to these practical/reflexive contexts, and it may be
that outside the interaction and dynamic of these situations
the ideas of the men's movement cannot be fully or sympa-
thetically appreciated. Certainly, to 'lift' ideas out of the context which has given rise to them and in which they have
specific meaning is to risk losing a sense of their significance
and purpose. The aim of the succeeding chapters is not to kill
a living body of ideas in order to categorize them and pursue
some kind of 'objective' strategy of analysis. The 'voices' with
which this chapter concludes are told as a way of giving
expression to the diversity and inter-active dynamic of men's
ongoing reconsideration of themselves as men.

The first two voices – Darren and Craig – are those of men
who are not involved in the men's movement or consciously

influenced by its ideas, but who nevertheless are asking questions about their identity and their relationships with women, and are living their lives in ways which are very different from those lived by their fathers. These voices describe some of the changes in men's role and identity which have followed on from the women's movement, and also from social changes in areas such as the economic profile of Britain and attitudes towards sexuality. The voices which follow are those of men who are influenced by different aspects of the men's movement: Daniel has links with the mythopoeic men's movement; Steve is part of a men's group which is committed to an anti-sexist stance and is allied to feminism; Andrew is part of a Christian men's group. In some ways these latter voices are those of men who have involved themselves with the men's movement as a way of responding to the massive shifts in men's role and identity which Darren and Craig are living out. In part the men's movement has been a way of coping with these changes, sharing the confusion and distress that has resulted from the challenges of new expectations – and for some men particularly in relationship with women (see Chapter 5). Yet the men's movement is also an expression of men's desire to embrace the possibility of reshaping roles, identity and relationships; there is an excitement and enthusiasm for this work in the company of other men, and an interplay of ideas and practise which issue in a range of developing life-styles and self-understandings.

However, if prophecies such as those of Virginia Woolf have read the signs of the times aright, and it is correct to suggest that this reflexive focus among men has arisen primarily in response to the women's movement and its challenge to the unjust power relations of patriarchy, then a crucial issue for the men's movement must be one of justice. For if men are seeking to redefine or rediscover themselves as men in response to women influenced by feminism, then it must be asked whether they are pursuing just forms of relations among themselves, and between themselves and women, as feminism demands. Of the many questions which men are asking themselves, we must ask ourselves one more:

to what extent are the ideas of men's studies tackling the issues of men's power in relation to women and one another, and how do they provide strategies which contribute for change towards a future in which there is justice for all?

Different voices

Darren

Darren is twenty-five. He has been married for four years to Sandy, who is thirty-four. They have two children: Peter, a boy aged eight who is Sandy's son from her previous marriage; and Sophie, a girl of four years. She is the reason they married, says Darren. They had been split up some months when Sandy told Darren that she was pregnant, after having lived with him for a year or so. Darren says that now he understands that he moved in with Sandy to escape from home, and that Sandy took to him as she had recently split from her drunk and abusive husband. Darren regrets the marriage, except that he feels Sophie is the best thing that has ever happened to him. He loves both the children, though the courts will not allow him to adopt Peter, who wants to retain his natural father. It is the children he works hard for, not himself. Being a father was not something he ever expected or planned, and yet he is happy to be one. The way both of the children cuddle up to him and tell him that they love him gives him a marvellous thrilling warmth. When Sandy tells him that she loves him he is unable to reply. He does not expect the marriage to last, but stays in order to give the children what they need. He feels that he has made his decisions and must pay the price.

Darren works in a steel-cutting factory, Sandy in a shop (where they first met). Darren's father and brother work at the factory, along with his uncles and male cousins. Darren hates the work but the money is good. He works twelve-hour shifts. His father is a team leader and adores the work. He is known as a hard gaffer. Darren was a team leader for a week's trial but hated it. His father wants him to get on in the place, but his only ambition is to get out when he can. But the shifts stop him

retraining at night school, and the money is better than anything else he could hope for. He has ideas for a novel in his
head – hundreds of plots, but there is no time to write. He says
hardly any of the men in the factory are happy at work, but
thousands of men have been dumped in the last few years and
it's a miracle to have a regular job.

On the factory floor it is all men. The atmosphere is macho:
football, swearing, competitions to prove physical strength.
Darren is sure that no one is interested in ideas. Most of the
men are married. Only a few (strange) characters remain
single, living with their mothers still and existing only for
work. There is a lot of racism and homophobia, lots of *Sun*
Page Three attitudes to women. Darren feels very much dis-
trusted because of his 'effeminate' style. He is insulted a lot by
the men, called 'poof' and 'queer'. He feels himself to have a
verbal and intellectual strength which is stronger than their
macho toughness: the names they call him don't disturb him.
It is something he has got used to through school. He feels that
he has become very tough and independent – this is how he
has to be to survive.

His father would bully him, too, wanting him to be like his
brother, who is a boxer. He hated Darren's quietness and
introspection, the way he spoke or dyed his hair or had his
ears pierced as a teenager. The family was very open about
sex. He and his brothers would watch his father's porn videos
when their parents were out. He could talk to his parents
about sex. But his father always wanted to make his sons into
'proper men': muscular and loud and 'on for a fight'. He felt a
great deal of pressure to live up to these expectations. Having
Sophie was the first thing in his life of which his father was
proud, Darren feels. It 'made a man of him'. His mother was
keen for him not to rush into marriage so early in life, but
Darren wanted to do the proper thing, be a proper father. That
is why he let his father find him the job at the factory. His
father has always been very involved in their upbringing, but
in ways which impose his own ideas of how his sons should
live their lives.

The work is physically demanding – a great deal of lifting,

pushing, heaving about. It has made Darren very much bigger and more muscular than he was as a teenager. That does not please him particularly. He does not feel that working with his father has in any way conformed him to his father's expectations. When Darren is on the machine cutting sheets of steel for hours on end the work bores him. He fantasizes about where else he might be and with whom. The 'splitting' is even harder work, cutting up long, large pieces of hot steel for industrial use. The men work in teams of four, producing forty tons of split steel a shift. There is no team spirit – lots of arguing and rivalry. If he can, Darren will take his break with his brother. His brother is the only man in the place who can string a sentence together, and they have always been close. Darren worshipped him as a boy. Since they both have serious relationships they have grown apart a little, but still keep in touch.

Darren shares the house work with Sandy. He does all the cooking, she cleans. They share the ironing and the shopping. Darren has to do the gardening. The neighbours would expect to see the man of the house mow the lawns. He hates the garden. Darren shares the care of Peter and Sophie with Sandy and his mother. They juggle who does what around work, family shifts as well as work shifts. If Darren is working at night, then he takes Sophie to school when he gets home in the morning and also collects her again in the afternoon, getting some sleep in between. Sandy works shop hours. They are buying their council house. They have two cars, a newly paved drive, lovely furniture, fashionable clothes, a foreign holiday every year. The children want for nothing; they are spoilt, Darren thinks. They are materialistic, insatiable in their demands, and never happy. This is his and Sandy's major fault: they are too materialistic as people, always striving for the next purchase, Sandy more so than him, Darren feels. She is pleased by the 'right' car, the 'right' jewellery, the 'right' label on clothes. Darren feels she wants him for what he can give her as much as anything else, like her father did for her and her mother. He feels that most men in his area are tamed by their wives, restricted by them into doing what women want by a fear of nagging and emotional fireworks. Men will do anything to avoid an argument. There are a few men on the estate who will get violent after a few drinks, and this might be to shut up the nagging.

Darren would like to live in the country, by the sea in North Wales where there are no shops to make the children want things, no danger from traffic or molesters to limit their play, nothing to make demands on him or Sandy. He feels his life is very constrained. He feels that men ought to stand up for themselves much more, that women manipulate them, that they let women make them into children again. Even so, most of the men he knows have got nothing going for them as people. They are slaves to convention. They fear what they do not understand. They understand very little which is beyond their limited experience. Most of them like it that way.

Craig

Craig grew up in the suburbs and went to a grammar school. Both his parents are professionals, as is his brother and sister. He went to university without really questioning whether he should or not, and spent most of his time there drinking and playing hockey. When he graduated he spent a year working abroad, and then came back to train as a social worker. Whilst studying on the course he met Sue, and they have lived together since – for seven years. They now have a child, Crispin, aged three. Soon after Crispin was born Craig gave up working full-time so that he could share the parenting, which Craig really enjoys – watching Crispin develop, taking him swimming and to playgroup, helping him learn. He was present at the birth and has been fully involved in Crispin's life since then. He is glad that times have changed since he was younger and saw very little of his own father. He does not resent this, or the fact that his parents were both so busy with their work. He feels times have changed, and that there is a lot more freedom now. He feels sorry for his own father because social convention kept him at work away from his family. He also feels that his mother had to work more than she would have liked in order to prove herself. He feels that he is gaining from the newer way of things, and that Crispin is benefitting too.

Sue and he are not married and see no reason why they ought to become so: their relationship is a matter for them only and not the business of others – especially their families (though both families have been very supportive, and helped them considerably with the costs of buying their flat and getting a home established). Sue also works part-time, and although money is tight, they both prefer to have time and energy to devote to Crispin and one another. They want to find their satisfaction in one another and in their own personal interests and not just through work. In the future, if they have another child – which may be quite soon – Craig would be quite happy to give up paid employment altogether and to stay home full-time. He does not imagine that this would be dreary or isolating, nor that this is something he ought to do so that Sue's career isn't hampered. He feels that being at home would suit his personality. Sue remembers her own mother being a 'depressed housewife'. Craig does his share of the housework – which is half of it, except ironing. He hates ironing. Craig prefers to do the cooking, and has become an expert in Asian cuisine. They make most decisions jointly, though Sue is better financially. They try to make sure that they have their own friends, and each have a week-end away by themselves with family or friends from time to time.

Craig does have dreams about what Crispin might be when he grows up: a champion mountain-biker or an intrepid conservationist working on a worthwhile project abroad! But he wants Crispin to be himself and do what he wants to do, whatever that is or whoever he needs to be. He wouldn't mind if Crispin turned out to be gay, or became a Buddhist monk – or even if he worked as a solicitor in the City! That would be OK too: it's up to him.

Daniel

Daniel moved to Seattle when his relationship with his first wife, Carol, broke up. This break-up was very painful and took a long time to get over. Though he had relationships with women afterwards it was several years before he could make a commitment again. He has been with Kate for five years now and he feels that they have a fine relationship. They plan to have children soon.

As soon as he got to Seattle he went into therapy as a way of coming to terms with some of what had happened with Carol. He was very angry: for years they had wrangled over this and that, and whatever he did never seemed to be right for her. He had been brought up in a fairly conventional way, within what he had thought of as a normal family; he went to university and then trained as a lawyer, worked very hard and tried to get a decent lifestyle together for Carol and himself. Carol worked hard too. They drifted apart, but the parting was acrimonious: Carol attacked his lack of feelings and attentiveness, his performance in bed, his obsession with work. By the time they split he had no confidence in himself as a person and had no idea what women wanted from a relationship.

Daniel's therapist mentioned Robert Bly's work to him, and as soon as he read *Iron John*, so many things fell in to place: he began to see that he had only been living a kind of half-life in which his emotions and longings as a man were suppressed. He had never really thought about being a man until he read Bly, but as soon as he did so he realized that there were so many unhealthy ways of being a man which he was continuing automatically. Now he can see that Carol was wanting him to 'come alive', and yet she was wanting him to become someone *she* created rather than encouraging him to be who he really was. Kate is very different.

Daniel's therapist gave him a contact for a men's group, to which he still belongs. They meet weekly to talk about all kinds of issues: their relationships, sexuality, work, children. Daniel's life has been transformed. He feels in touch with his body, and he is no longer afraid of intimacy with other men. He feels that he has a much more healthy attitude to work, his emotions, and that his life has much more of a stable pattern to it. The most amazing part of the group's life was when they attended a camp by the sea together, which was facilitated by a very gifted man who led them for three days on what was a journey 'into themselves'. Daniel feels that this was a spiritual experience as much as anything, a time which helped them to make contact with a kind of energy deep down, a primitive power which is linked with all creatures and with the planet. There was drumming and dancing and singing around the camp fire, and a wonderful group bonding as they spent the days and nights together. He feels that for the first time in his life he has come to understand what being a man is truly about, a unity of body, mind and spirit, and that all the old macho stuff is a travesty. He has learned to accept the power of his feelings, his need for intimacy with other men and also his need for solitude. Kate encourages him in all of this and doesn't think he's a weirdo when he wants to go off into the wilderness by himself or wants to spend time with other men.

A powerful thing that happened for Daniel has been the healing of his relationship with his father. During the camp there was time for the members of the group to go back over their boyhoods and connect with feelings of being neglected by their fathers. There was a great deal of grief among the men because of their poor relationships with their fathers – how they were unable to talk with them, be physical or emotional with them, feel any kind of close affinity with them. There was a massive fear among some of them that they would repeat their own fathers' failings and become strangers to their own sons. To accept this 'father wound' was very painful for Daniel, but also a wonderful breakthrough. He was able to let all his anger and sorrow go as he wept with the other men. This was a transformative experience. It was part of his becoming an adult male, a 'real man', what some people call 'initiatory'. Since then he has slowly begun to build a new kind of relationship with his father, and he is pleased that in many ways they have become friends.

Now he feels that the life which he led was power-driven and heartless, and that in his first marriage his wife exploited the poverty of his masculinity. She was much stronger as a person, as a woman, than he was as a man. Daniel feels that he knows what he wants out of relationships, and what he is able to bring as a man, rather than just having to respond to a woman's lead.

Steve

Since he was at college Steve has been very much a 'group person'; he was involved with student politics, with the Lesbian and Gay Society and with numerous groups since, including two men's groups. He feels that maybe he would like to be less group-focussed in the future, but that the men's group will remain part of his life. The present group contains a variety of men. Two are currently unemployed, but all are middle class and white. Steve is bi-sexual, and two of the men are gay and the other four are straight. The group has talked about sexuality a great deal, and Steve feels that some members have had difficulty accepting homosexuality, though it took time for them to come clean about this. Some of the straight members were obsessed with what two men did in bed together, which brought up a lot of stuff about how sex is linked in with power. This caused the straight men to think about their own sexual behaviour. Steve wonders if these men are now better lovers! One man, who is married, acknowledged that his own sexuality is ambivalent – something with which the group had helped him to face. It feels really good to Steve that men are talking openly with one another about sex in a way that is safe and creative.

Generally the group is very accepting and supportive, though this has evolved as members have learnt to deal with conflict and difference. One of the good things about the group is that it has helped members to deal with anger and conflict in new and constructive ways. It has also helped men to tackle the issues of work and competitivism, drinking, body image and self-worth, emotions and how to handle them, parenting, and relationships with women and with other men. The purpose of the group is to try and work out new ways of being men which are appropriate for the diversity and flexibility of today; to explore what the stereotypes do to men and to get beyond them.

At the outset, and for a long time, the members were expressing a lot of confusion about what 'being a man' might mean now. In Steve's previous men's group there was a lot of focus on men's relationship to women, which Steve felt often bordered on guilt: an apology for being men, and an obsession with becoming acceptable to women – particularly hard-line feminists with whom one or two of the men seemed to be involved. Steve feels that the present group is more use to him because it goes beyond this obsession with what women think about men, partly because it includes other men such as himself who are not in partnerships with women. Issues connected with women are just part of what the group is about, and the special thing about a group is that men differ and that big abstract social issues always take on a different meaning when they come down to the particulars of an individual's life and relationships.

Andrew

Andrew is fifty-three and has been married to Celia since he was twenty-four. They have three children, one of whom is still living at home. The family live in Surrey; Andrew is an accountant, and they have 'a very comfortable' existence. Andrew was brought up as a Christian, attended a boarding-school which had strong Evangelical links and worshipped in an Evangelical church whilst at university. Both he and Celia are fully involved in their local parish church, where Andrew is the treasurer. Another member of the church, a much younger family man, invited Andrew to be part of a men's group based at the church, and to his surprise Andrew has found this group an immensely enriching part of his life for the last two years.

Andrew looks back and wonders whether its initial appeal wasn't harking back to his younger days at school and college – the fervour of Christian Union and the special friendships he had as a young man with other men, but which has lapsed through family responsibilities and the pressure of work. Andrew sees that it was partly these very pressures which were gnawing away at him inside that made him welcome the group so much. He has found a closeness and an openness with the other men in the group which he has never experienced before, mainly because some of the younger men have moved the group on into areas which he was not used to discussing. There have been conversations about men's feelings for women other than their wives and about some problems with the sexual side of one man's marriage. Andrew has been able to share some of his worries about his youngest son (who is having a difficult adolescence), and also some of his anxieties about getting older, losing his energy and enthusiasm for life, finding work unsatisfying or over-demanding, the relevance of faith to some of these questions.

The men in the group meet at varying times – sometimes before work for a prayer breakfast, or during an evening, or on special occasions like the picnic they have planned for their families – and they pray together about issues which they have shared. Andrew has been amazed at how much trust and frankness has developed among these men, and is impressed that church can be about friendship and personal issues. It has brought his faith alive again, and helped revitalize his relationship with Celia – just by having a place where he can talk and listen with other men, and also because some of the subjects in the group have made him reflect on aspects of who he is as a man and what is appropriate behaviour for him towards Celia and the children. He has been able to give advice and to learn from other men. The man who initiated the group receives material from various men's movements in the United States, and Andrew has studied these, some of which he finds a little too earnest and conservative for his 'English' tastes. But he does feel that the church has to make a place for men to be men and that it should reach out to men who are isolated or confused by all the pressures of modern life. The church needs to take seriously the pressures on men who are overworked and who want to be genuine fathers and loving husbands.

4

Rediscovering the Deep Masculine

Of all the literature concerning masculinity, Robert Bly's book *Iron John* has received the most public attention on both sides of the Atlantic. Bly is one of a clutch of North American writers who have developed an emphasis on issues concerning men and masculinity. Bly is a poet and a lecturer, a translator, story-teller and 'spiritual provocateur' whose ideas on masculinity first found widespread publicity in an interview published in *New Age* magazine in 1982. Bly roots himself in the Platonic tradition of Western philosophy, in the poetry of Blake, Yeats, D. H. Lawrence and Rilke. His writing and thinking are profoundly influenced by Carl Jung, and his colleagues are the Jungian analysts and psychotherapists of North America: James Hillman, Robert Moore and Keith Thompson (who first interviewed Bly in 1982). These authors have undertaken to respond to what they perceive as a crisis in men in Western society, offering the insights of Jungian psychoanalytical theory and practice. For Jung, to use the words of his disciple Frieda Fordham, the unconscious 'is not merely a cellar where man (humanity) dumps his rubbish, but the source of consciousness and of the creative and destructive spirit of mankind'.[1] The unconscious feeds, nourishes and invades the conscious mind and behaviour of men and women in every society and context. For Bly, the contemporary American crisis amongst men – the psychological breakdown, physical sickness, crime, violence, addiction, and general dysfunction that seem to have reached epidemic proportions in American society – has its causes and solutions at source, on the deep level of the unconscious.

In Jungian understanding, myths are a direct expression of

the collective unconscious, and through the ancient stories and archetypal images contained in them the needs and patterns of the human psyche can be discerned and adhered to. These stories are the source of human healing on an individual and corporate level: 'Stories, then – fairy stories, legends, myths, hearth stories – amount to a reservoir where we keep new ways of responding that we can adopt when the conventional and current ways run out.'[2] So for example, Robert Johnson's *He: Understanding Masculine Psychology* interprets the story of Parsifal's search for the holy grail as the unfolding of a path which each man must take in order to come to 'mature masculinity' and personal integration. This is not to imply that the Jungian writers are setting out to impose a rigid definition of masculinity, nor is it their aim to put forward a precise and correct vision of how men are to be. Amplifying Bly's thinking in a reader on men's issues, Keith Thompson talks of 'masculinities', and is keen, through a variety of representative texts in his collection, to show that the expressions in men of the 'deep masculine' to which Bly *et al.* point are diverse and multifarious: 'intrinsically plural ... mixed, complex, ambiguous'.[3]

Bly sees the present time as a moment of opportunity for men as well as a time of crisis. It is a time of deep psychic pain, of neurosis, in which men are spiritually undernourished and aimless on a profound level, without guidance or direction: 'the images of adult manhood given by popular culture are worn out; a man can no longer depend on them', Bly says in his opening sentence. This is a realization which men in the West begin to come to in their mid-thirties and onwards, once they have begun to establish themselves in a career and relationships. Bly finds that men are seeking self-understanding and fulfilment, that there is a kind of male grief and anguish in the Western industrialized cultures, a sense of loss which has developed since men ceased working on the land and lost touch with nature and the primitive culture which fostered healthy communities. According to Bly, modern men are continually seeking new models for themselves; they have moved away from the macho man image of the 1950s, through the tempestuous stage of the 1960s and 1970s, to a period in which women are in the ascendant, a time when men have learnt from women to embrace their 'feminine' aspects. Now men are able to listen to others, empathize, experience emotion; they are life-preserving, anti-war, pro-ecology; they have become what Bly terms 'soft men' who are able to relate to their female counterparts, and yet – in comparison with them – are limp, listless, needy, incomplete. Men have no mentors as they used to have in the primitive, pre-industrial cultures. Boys are separated from their fathers and mature men by the structures of modern social life in which male adulhood is spent in the office, away from the children. Boys are not fathered, they have no one to initiate them into manhood, no rituals of danger and pain through which to break from the dependencies of boyhood and make the deep, psychic transition into manhood. So boys attempt to initiate themselves, through drugs, violence, crime – by any means of danger or hurt which will give them the scar their subconscious longs for. Grown men have no true sense of what masculinity is, no sense of how to be a man. Men are disconnected from the masculine energies deep within themselves which all men share.

> When a contemporary man looks down into his psyche, he may, if conditions are right, find under the water of his soul, lying in an area no one has visited for a long time, an ancient hairy man. The mythological systems associate hair with the instinctive and the sexual and the primitive ... every modern male has, lying at the bottom of his psyche, a large, primitive being covered with hair down to his feet. Making contact with this Wild Man is the step the Eighties male or the Nineties male has yet to take.[4]

So Bly turns to the story of Iron John and 'finds' within this tale eight stages or movements which comprise an 'initiatory path' for men whereby they attain the full dignity and integrity of the 'deep masculine'. The story is of a kingdom in which there is a forest. Men travelling in the forest have mysteriously failed to return. One day a knight from a far land comes into the kingdom and asks the king for dangerous, heroic work (as knights do). The king tells him about the problem with the forest. The knight enters the forest with his dog. In the midst of the forest he finds a pool. As they travel past the pool an arm emerges from the water and grasps the poor dog, dragging him down into the depths. The knight leaves the forest and fetches men to help him drain the water out of the pool, bucket by bucket. At the bottom of the pool they find a man, a wild man, covered with reddish hair. This is Iron John (red being the colour of iron). The knight takes Iron John to the king, who locks him up in an iron cage in the courtyard of the castle, giving the key to his wife. The queen puts this key safely under her pillow.

The king's son is playing ball in the courtyard. His ball is a golden ball, and it rolls into the iron cage. The imprisoned wild man will only return the ball to the prince if he goes to fetch the key from under his mother's pillow and releases him. The boy does this, and he goes off with Iron John into the forest, fleeing the anger of his parents. In the forest the boy plays by a magical stream and gains wonderful golden hair. He must then leave the forest and finds dirty work in the kitchens and gardens of the castle of a foreign king. Here he meets the daughter of the king. The golden-haired young man proves himself to be a heroic warrior through the help of Iron John, to whom he returns when he is in need. The foreign king, astounded by the beauty, wealth and skill of the young prince, gives him the hand of his daughter in marriage. His father and mother attend the wedding, overjoyed that they have found their son again. To the wedding comes a splendid king, who embraces the prince and reveals himself to be Iron John, who through a spell had been turned into the wild man. The prince has freed him from that enchantment, and so Iron John bestows on him all his wealth. The End.

Bly's interpretation of this tale is that the wild man in the story is *the* Wild Man, an archetypal figure of the masculine unconscious. Bly believes that men in the Western world have to make contact with this Wild Man if they are to fulfil their

longings to regain the dignity and splendour of being men.
The Wild Man is not the Savage Man of violence and destructiveness who seems to be wreaking havoc among contemporary men in crime, drugs and violence. The Wild Man will lead
men into those innate qualities of masculinity such as 'the
spontaneity we have preserved from childhood', a 'genuine
friendliness toward the wildness in nature', a willingness to
'leave the busy life'. The Wild Man will enable men to embrace
'the positive side of male sexuality' and engage with the emotions, needs, desires and darkness of the inner psychological
self. Bly's interpretation of the Iron John story is to show men
how to root themselves in the true, essential man within, to
tap ancient energies, for 'the structure at the bottom of the
male psyche is still as firm as it was twenty thousand years
ago. A contemporary man simply has very little help getting
down to it.'[5]

Hence the range of organizations, workshops, therapists
and literature which is now available to help men 'get down'
to 'the deep nourishing and spiritually radiant energy' which
in men is to be found 'not in the feminine side, but in the deep
masculine'.[6] The aspect of this men's movement which has
received most media attention – the resort of groups of men to
the wilderness of woods to participate in bonding rituals and
to make contact with their buried hurts, fears and longings as
men – is motivated by Bly's view that men are kept away from
the 'nourishing dark' within themselves by the commercial,
militarist culture of the West. Bly does not list secularism as an
obstacle for men's rediscovery of themselves in this 'deep'
sense, but he does regard Christianity as a hindrance, so far as
churches continue to preach niceness and docility and a vision
of Jesus meek and mild which gives no initiation into 'male
spirit':

It is good that the divine is associated with the Virgin Mary
and a blissful Jesus, but we can sense how different it would
be for a young man if we lived in a culture where the divine
also was associated with mad dancers, fierce fanged men
and a being entirely underwater, covered with hair.[7]

Bly does point admiringly to the wild Christ overturning the tables in the temple, but laments the nice Jesus of the Western churches and their lack of a place for the representation and celebration of male sexual energy, the absence of what he understands Pan, Dionysus, Hermes and Shiva to represent in other religious systems. Christ is problematic for Bly: he is wifeless, childless and effectively sexless. He does not see in Jesus of Nazareth the saviour whom contemporary men need. Bly draws on the conviction of the analyst von Franz that the male psyche, and the female psyche too, is longing for a new saviour figure, one whom she finds recurring in the dreams of her clients – 'a religious figure but a hairy one, in touch with God and sexuality, with spirit and earth'.[8] The Jesus of Christian cult is represented as wet even though he is bearded: he is not a hairy man from the underwater world! For Bly, Christianity, together with Judaism and Islam, are predominantly anti-erotic and therefore damaging to men and women alike. The feminist critique that these religions have banished *Eros* has been taken up from the male perspective by Bly and his followers.

Whilst Bly's approach is clearly appealing to some men, others will find his metaphors for the 'deep masculine' somewhat strange, unhelpful or irrelevant to their concerns. Some suspect Bly of the rugged individualism that men have found so disabling to emotional expression and relationships in the past. It may be that men are not as much in touch with their 'feminine side' as Bly assumes, nor as comfortable in relationships with women, nor as convinced by the mythopoeic approach to psychoanalytical theory. Though a reinforcement of the isolation, obsessive control and violence of traditional masculine stereotypes is certainly not what Bly intends, the Wild Man, Warrior, King approach to male identity smacks too much of these – particularly for women. And because so much of the current debates about masculinity has arisen in response to feminism, women's response is crucial. Bly's point is that men have now exhausted themselves in their attempts to re-shape themselves in response to feminism; yet many men are seeking a masculine identity which feels both authentic in

its maleness and in its capacity to sustain equitable relationships with women and other men.

A rather more wide-ranging book which draws together
sociological, ecological and mythopoeic themes is Sam Keen's
Fire in the Belly. As in *Iron John*, men are encouraged to set out
on a spiritual/psychological journey of healing and integration, but Keen makes it much more explicit that this is both a
personal and a cultural, social movement. Like Bly, Keen
offers a critique of the present culture which sets about
constructing a liberationist ontology for men in the light of
feminism. Keen asserts that in the present culture, in which
feminism is in the ascendant, men feel 'blamed, demeaned
and attacked'.[9] The modes of life available to men – the 'Rites
of Man' being war, work, and sex – only serve to impoverish,
delude and alienate them. The harm done to men in and
through these structures distorts their relationship with
women and with one another. Men need to find an identity
and a dignity which is not bound up with the obligations of
defence and the preparedness for violence, the measurement
of personal success and achievement exclusively through
work, and the supposed ever-ready potency and predatori-
ness of masculine sexual desire. Keen asserts that men 'are
violent because of the systematic violence done to their bodies
and spirits. Being hurt they become hurters';[10] and that they
will have to accept the need to retain their capacity to defend
themselves and others in an imperfect world, yet without
being pro-actively violent and aggressive themselves. He carefully maps out the unwritten rules of commercial culture to
show how these operate to define men as 'economic man', disconnected from the natural world and even the actual physical processes of manufacture, making him sedentary, amoral,
isolated and friendless, desensitized – 'the creature who
defines itself within the horizons of work and consumption …
a being who has been neutralized, degendered, rendered sub-
servient to the laws of the market'.[11] Keen analyses the
sterotypes of men's (heterosexual) attitudes and practices
regarding sex – their phallic obsessionism and conquest/per-
formance idealism – to suggest that 'men's private experience

of sex is vastly different from the usual stereotypes, is as complex as women's, and is as filled with longing for intimacy and spiritual meaning'.[12] Young men need the responsible guidance of fathers and mentors, and to learn to be less frantic in their sexual relationships. Keen reinterprets men's posturing and crass obsessiveness with sex as an emphasis on the only activity in which men have 'cultural permission' for intimacy: 'Listen with the third ear and you can hear a sacred intent beneath the façade of even the most vulgar language. Emotionally speaking, men are stutterers who often use sexual language to express their forbidden desires for communion.'[13]

Keen suggests that a new vision of manhood is necessary, an ontological shift and a transformation of purpose which is appropriate to contemporary needs and opportunities; men must find a new *vocation* – a renewed task and a renewed identity: 'The historical challenge for men is clear – to discover a peaceful form of virility and to create an ecological commonwealth, to become fierce gentlemen.'[14] In this perspective the present time of anguish and turmoil for men becomes a process of creative possibility – if men are prepared to abandon their outmoded and oppressive ways of being for the spiritual quest and the free-flowing life of the imagination. Keen urges men to become 'pilgrims', to embark on a process of ongoing existential questioning, to set out on an inner journey of self-discovery which will enable a movement from individualism, compulsive activity, the evasion of fears and feelings, from the false securities of macho norms, military might and technological domination, from the domination of guilt and shame, toward a renewal in community, but also solitude and 'fallowness', in the facing of fears and the acceptance of doubts, toward co-operative ways of working and an ecological consciousness. Keen suggests that the virtues of the 'new, heroic man', the 'fierce gentleman' to be born out of this process, are those which might be described as wonder, empathy, a 'heartful mind' (reflectiveness and self-acceptance), moral outrage, the capacity for enjoyment, friendship, communion, 'husbanding' (the actions of caring and commitment), and 'wildness' (which Keen interprets as a familiarity with the non-urban environment). Such 'gentlemen' will seek justice and right relationship rather than war and exploitation.

The 'fierceness' of these men is to be about having firmness and anger in their present traumatic struggle with women. Keen stresses that this fierceness is not violence, but an inner strength in the face of the accusations made against them by feminism. Men experience 'undifferentiated guilt in the presence of women',[15] and it is men's 'impotence' in this situation which leads them to 'resort to' violence. Keen urges men to develop a discerning approach to feminism: to find in some feminism a 'prophetic' protest – a call to repentance and a model for change, but to resist in 'ideological feminism' the politics of the 'genderal blame game' in which women heap unjust accusations upon men, just as women have been held responsible for all the evils of the world in the past by men. Keen argues that this 'switch in the dialectics of blame' must be replaced by an honest examination of how both women and men have been 'enslaved' in an iniquitous system which has crippled both, and in which both have colluded. The new vocation is for men and women to work together for a new world of harmony through a process of personal and corporate metanoia:

> The healing of the relationship between the sexes will not begin until men and women cease to use their suffering as a justification for their hostility. It serves no useful purpose to argue about who suffers most. Before we can begin again together, we must repent separately. In the beginning we need simply to listen to each other's stories, the histories of wounds. Then we must examine the social-economic-political system that has turned the mystery of man and woman into the alienation between the genders. And, finally, we must grieve together. Only repentance, mourning, and forgiveness will open our hearts to each other and give us the power to begin again.[16]

Keen, much more than Bly, offers the location for this healing. The nuclear family is understood as the place in which the *mystery* of man and woman unfolds, may be explored and redeemed: 'marriage and family may provide the best hospital for our ancient wounds'.[17] He is much more explicit than Bly about the relational benefits of a man's spiritual quest, and envisages that most men will undertake this journey either prior to or within or in the ruins of a marital relationship. Keen seeks to re-integrate the family and fatherhood into the heart of masculine values, for 'beneath the façade of socially constructed differences between men and women, there is a genuine mystery of biological and ontological differences', an opposition for which marriage provides complementarity, 'ineradicable differences' which may be celebrated and cherished within the procreation of children.[18] It is in fatherhood that men may find themselves healed of 'our wound and our longing for the missing father' who was absent through work or banished by his fear of intimacy;[19] men may find wholeness by becoming for their children the father they longed for themselves. It is within a renewed participation in the family, and through a new understanding of and commitment to the family, that most men will discover a new and fulfilling virility.

Women respond to the 'men's movement'

The feminist theologian Rosemary Radford Ruether is emphatic that power is the fundamental issue which men must tackle in any attempt to understand themselves and redefine their relationships with women and one another:

> Patriarchy is itself the original Men's Movement, and the struggle to overthrow it must be a movement of men as well as women. But men can only authentically be part of that strugle if they are able to acknowledge the injustice of their own historical privilege as males and to recognize the ongoing ideologies and economic, political, and social structures that keep such privilege in place.
>
> In short, men must begin by acknowledging their public reality as males in patriarchal society, and not retreat to a

privatized self that avoids accountability for a public world. They must see that the private self is not an autonomous entity, but a dependent appendage of these social power relations.[20]

Exposed to this criticism, the men's movement characterized by Bly's work would seem less than satisfactory to feminists. Indeed, some regard it as retrogressive and dangerous. Bly's theories, and the mythopoeic approach as a whole, have been criticized as a vehicle for the renovation of abusive male power under the guise of reformed identity, particularly where men adopt these theories without a recognition of male power as it currently operates under patriarchy. The American feminists Jane Gaputi and Gordene Makenzie have called Iron John 'an archetype of antagonistic masculinity', a representation of maleness which is 'narrowness, inequality and emnity', an image of man defined as not-woman. They reject Iron John as a transformative metaphor for men, arguing that a man of *iron* represents inflexible, confining, enslaving masculinity, and that the archetypal images of Warrior and King which furnish the psychologies of the men's movement are typologies which reinforce conventional gender roles, reimprisoning men and reasserting male domination of women.[21]

Gloria Steinem suggests that both women and men should not only interrogate the language of the men's movement but go on to ask whether its ideas and concepts will bring about social transformation in the diminution of violence by men against women, in enabling men to cross the present barriers of race, sexuality and gender, and by encouraging men to take more genuine participation in and responsibility for the care of children.[22] In the United States, where enthusiasm for discovering the Wild Man is strongest, pro-feminist men such as Stoltenberg have rejected the privatizing asocial tendencies they perceive in Robert Bly and those who draw on his work.[23] He suspects that the conservative Men's Rights lobby and fundamentalist Christian moralists are lurking in the shadow of the Wild Man.

Michael Jacobs has suggested that 'new men' are in danger of intruding on women's ground, interfering in business which is properly that of women and the women's movement.[24] This might be so where men are in some sense attempting to supervise feminism or to pre-empt the implications of an honest response to its criticisms by purporting to change whilst retaining male power intact – and it is here that Gloria Steinem's assessment is important for safeguarding the integrity of men as well as continuing to pursue the feminist agenda of change in society. The enterprise of men facing up to the realities of their power and its implications for women and for themselves in particular situations and with reference to specific behaviours is fraught with difficulty. Men's vision may be clouded with denial and evasion, and they might well seek social theories which endorse their power – ideas such as those suggesting it is in some sense 'natural' for men to be violent when angry.[25] The exploration of masculinity might be such an evasion writ large. From an American context, Kathleen Carlin, a woman involved in a shelter for battered women and a worker with violent men in 'batterer's groups', sees the homosocial separatism implied in the men's movement as indicative of a flight from women and the implications of the women's movement. In her view men will never come to a transformative understanding of masculinity whilst they ignore women in the process, without whom masculinity has no meaning. Men have to listen to others, and in doing so embrace the need for radical change in gender relations:

> The decision to give up male centrality, to listen to those who have been marginalized, to be willing to perceive a broader, richer reality than male supremacy offers, means giving up all forms of controlling and abusive behaviour and learning new skills with which to negotiate the intricate, demanding transition which lies ahead.[26]

From Carlin's perspective, one which is shaped by experience of the 'dark side' of men, new ways of men being men will only come if created in community with women. This process will involve men in 'de-centring' themselves, shifting the primary focus from male needs and desires to an attentiveness to the experiences of women, and making appropriate life choices and policy decisions in response. This is not so much the accession to a masculine 'kingship', but abdication – what Carlin describes as a 'defection from patriarchy', a defection in which each man must understand that 'to save himself means not grasping patriarchy closer, but letting it die – even the part of it that resides within himself'.[27]

This fundamental critique of the men's movement being articulated by women in the United States – that it evades the realities of men's power over women – is very much borne in mind by those men who can be grouped together as 'constructionist' in approach. An analysis of male power is a key theme in constructionist approaches to men and masculinity.

5

Reconstructing Men and Masculinity

> The starting point of critical elaboration is the consciousness
> of what one really is, and is 'knowing thyself' as a product
> of the historical process to date which has deposited in you
> an infinity of traces, without leaving an inventory.
>
> (Antonio Gramsci)[1]

In presenting some of the constructionist approaches to the
study of men and masculinity, this chapter focusses on the
theory of gender as a means for understanding and transforming men's relationships – between men, and between
men and women. In particular, the autobiographical nature of
some writing about masculinity shows how a critical awareness of gender by men moves beyond analysis towards the
social reconstruction of masculinity.

Masculinity as an aspect of gender relations

In her book *Slow Motion*, which explores social change among
men from a feminist perspective, Lynne Segal writes not about
'masculinity', but about 'masculinities'. Like many of the col-
lections of essays which 'unmask' or deconstruct masculinity,
Segal makes a study of the various ways of being a man in
relation to class, race, sexuality and social culture: Black
masculinities, gay, anti-sexist, macho and so on.[2] Segal asserts
that the differences between men are crucial because they
reveal that

> the force and power of the dominant ideas of masculinity ...
> do not derive from any intrinsic characteristic of indivi-
> duals, but from the social meanings which accrue to those

ideals from their supposed superiority to that which they
are not. To be 'masculine' is *not* to be 'feminine', *not* to be
'gay', *not* to be tainted with any marks of 'inferiority' –
ethnic or otherwise.[3]

Masculinity is not uniform, but multifarious; it is not innate,
but is grounded in bodily experience and created through
social interaction in which difference – between men and men
and men and women – is related to power and hierarchy.
From this perspective masculinity is

> neither biologically determined nor a simple product of
> social stereotypes and expectations. It is a complex and
> difficult process of psychic construction, ineluctably marked
> by tension, anxiety and contradiction. It has no single and
> consistent set of attributes and essence.[4]

The generative force behind much constructionist writing is
to deconstruct conventional masculinities which, these writers
would suggest, are a denial of the fluidity and relationality of
manhood. They seek to expose what Anthony Easthope calls
'the masculine myth':

> Masculinity aims to be one substance all the way through.
> In order to do this it must control what threatens it from
> within and without. Within, femininity and male homo-
> sexual desire must be denied; without, women and the
> feminine must be subordinated and held in place.[5]

In Easthope's analysis, under patriarchy the convention of a
fixed and homogenous masculinity seeks to deny the social
nature of identity and the 'lamination of desire' that go to
make up the shifting internal structures of self-in-relationship.
For him, psychoanalytical theory reveals that within the
unconscious of any individual there is a play between masculine and feminine, between heterosexual desire and homosexual desire. Yet the masculine myth denies this dynamic and
blinds men to the diversity of self, entrapping them in a con-

tinual struggle to promote the socially produced images and expectations of manhood: 'the burden of having to be one sex all the way through'.[6]

In its simplest form, the figures of boyhood fun such as Superman or the Incredible Hulk build into the developing male the notions of maleness as solitary, controlling, invulnerable. The ideals of athleticism in the icons of competitive sport or in Michelangelo's David suggest for Easthope the presiding notion that men must be aggressive, powerful and competitive. It is an ideal of internal repression and external domination, but one which, Easthope emphasizes, is beginning to slip. Men can no longer sustain its burdens, nor do they wish to. Men are seeking gender salvation, realizing that they are also victims within the present patriarchal regime in which they are enslaved as 'real men': unable to enjoy intimacy and accept the diversity of human sexuality, or admit to physical weakness and emotional need. Writers such as Easthope aim to show how these oppressive models of masculinity are built through social norms and operate at the deepest levels within men, affecting every aspect of their lives. This is what Bob Connell has described as 'hegemonic masculinity', under the rule of which social relations are ordered to the advantage of men within a regime which defines conventional masculinity as predominantly white, and male desire as compulsorily heterosexual. Masculinities which challenge or subvert the norm – such as those of gay men – are marginalized.[7]

Yet the theorization of masculinity is a field in which 'rival knowledges' compete. From his sociological perspective, Bob Connell has outlined the epistemological difficulties in forming a science of masculinity which is true to biological, sociological, philosophical and psychological perspectives. The sciences do not present a coherent theory of masculinity: the idea that men are defined and 'driven' by their biology and anatomy is in contradiction to the perceptions of the social sciences that masculinities are wholly the product of social influences and cultural norms – almost as if masculinity were projected on to bodies socially designated as 'male'. Taken in isolation, discreet scientific approaches are reductionist and

partial. An understanding of masculinity which has a place for
the formative importance of social and cultural influences
whilst simultaneously having an awareness of how the social
practice of masculinity is grounded in and formed by men's
bodies and minds seems elusive.[8]

What the sciences do emphasize, however, is that masculinity has meaning only in relation to femininity. Masculinity
is increasingly understood therefore as a construct of gender
relations:

> Masculinity and femininity are inherently relational con-
> cepts, which have meaning in relation to each other, as a
> social demarcation and a cultural opposition. This holds
> regardless of the changing content of the demarcation in
> different societies and periods of history. Masculinity as an
> object of knowledge is always masculinity-in-relation …
> Knowledge of masculinity arises within the project of know-
> ing gender relations.[9]

Thus the variety of masculinities lived by men may be
understood as *gender projects*[10] which are played out in relation
to one another and to the variety of 'the feminine' within any
particular time and culture.

Perhaps one of the cultural shifts which most characterizes
the present time is this heightened consciousness of gender.
The theory of gender now suggests that all aspects of human
culture may be 'read' as expressions or embodiments of the
relation between women and men and the inter-relation
between women and women, men and men. All human life
and thought may be interpreted as 'gendered'. Even the very
roots of Western thought, with its ancient binary conceptions
of good and bad, flesh and spirit, body and mind, feeling and
rationality, may be understood to lie in the perceived sexual
differences of maleness and femaleness.

In her recent book exploring the relationship between
gender, theology and the community of the church, Elaine
Graham has shown that gender is not a fixed conception, but
a shifting notion of developing theory. In the early part of this

century in the West, the behavioural qualities of masculinity and femininity were equated with biological sex. Then came the notion that gender was culturally conditioned, a product of 'sex role stereotyping' through the social institutions of family, school, the media and so on. Maleness was not solely dependent on the biological presence of a penis and testicles: masculinity was a learned set of values and behaviours. Biological sex thus came to be differentiated from a culturally imposed gender identity, and the idea of androgyny then developed in the 1970s. This is the notion that human personality incorporates both masculine and feminine 'aspects' which are not prescribed by physiology or biological sex, and that social roles and expectations could endorse this separation of biological sex from gender. Men were understood to have both a masculine and a feminine 'side': they could subdue their masculine traits and develop (or 'get in touch with') their feminine side to achieve a balanced personality.

Such a notion has come to be seen as implicitly dualistic in its distinction between biological and psychological identity. The androgynous ideal 'disembodies' the human person and thus denies the integration of the physical and biological with the psychological aspects which together contribute to the human conception of 'self'.

Sexual identity is now interpreted as a multiplicity of factors – social, biological, psychological, preferential – configurations of which take on a gendered significance in relation to other configurations. Gender has come to be theorized as part of the socio-linguistic structures which construct our self-understanding and perceptions of the world. Gender relations are seen as integral to the fundamental processes and structures of human culture and society.[11] From this perspective, men have begun to see their lives and perceptions not as normative or universal, the standard from which women, gay men or black men deviate, but as *male* – that is, specific to men's bodily, sexual and cultural experience. If men's lives are conceived as fluid 'gender projects' always formed and understood in relation to women and other men, rather than the outworkings of a fixed masculine nature, then they are open to comparison, analysis and change. This can be seen at its clearest in the autobiographical nature of men's study of themselves.

Critical autobiography

A man who writes will write from his own perspective as a man, and will therefore be saying something about himself as a man – his sense of masculinity: his text is gendered. In particular, autobiography by men may be read as expressions of masculine identity and practice. The *Confessions* of Augustine, Rousseau and Tolstoy, and Wordsworth's *Prelude*, may be read as oblique personal histories of masculinity. Men have written more expressly about the development of masculine identity through exploring the father-son relationship, as Kafka does in his *Letter to my Father*, and Edmund Gosse in *Father and Son*, and Blake Morrison in the book written in response to the death of his father, *And When Did You Last See Your Father?*. Gay men have explored masculine identity as an adjunct of telling their stories of growing-up gay, in books such as Edmund White's *A Boy's Own Story* and Michael Carson's *Sucking Sherbert Lemons* (books which also focus on the relationship between father and son). All these works articulate different aspects of male experience and different perspectives on masculinity – indeed, differing masculinities.

More recently, men have written about themselves in a way which demonstrates an awareness of gender relations. In *Unmasking Masculinity* David Jackson sets out to write a 'critical autobiography' which makes his personal history an exploration of masculine identity as it takes shape in particular times and circumstances. He understands the process of telling as a kind of liberating testimony, for in the narrative disclosure of his sense of self as a man – built up through boyhood, adolescence and adulthood, lived out in emotional, sexual and social relationship – this accrued masculinity is made open for examination and change. This is autobiography as deconstruction, the making apparent of the reality of social relationship, a process of 'felt, critical stocktaking that often leads to changed ways of relating and acting, and helps to develop a commitment to changing men in their social world'.[12]

So, for example, in the section 'Falling Apart' Jackson gives his account of how men's sense of self is represented or 'embodied' in his physique and body image. As a boy Jackson made great efforts to be a 'He-man', to be seen as strong and omnicompetent. His failure to achieve impossible standards left him with gnawing low self-esteem. He battled to impose his will over his body in sport and by pursuing a punishing performance ethic at work. This struggle led eventually to a heart attack, hospitalization and the terror of powerlessness and loss of control as a patient, and then the 'falling apart', a psychological collapse and the rejection of any more 'thrusting, driving, pushing … '.[13] In telling the story in the way he does, Jackson hopes to come over as more than an exceptional workaholic, unfulfilled husband and failed father who has seen the error of his unhealthy ways. He is attempting to draw attention to the social constructions of masculinity which damage men and distort their relationships, with the purpose of reforming masculine roles and identities. His aim is to encourage men to anchor their identities in aspects of their lives other than their work, and to resist allowing it to become their main source of self-esteem and personal achievement.

Jackson's reflections on his experience of fatherhood, and on his relationship with his own father, emphasize how the social prescriptions for masculinity have their personal implications, and how these private experiences – critically examined – bring about demands for public transformation. His personal reflections bring to the surface the more general need for fathers to have meaningful and creative involvement with their children, and for men to learn ways of being intimate with one another. The visits to his dying father in hospital seem to sum up for Jackson the power of the dominant culture to deny two men, however closely linked, the joy of intimacy, emotional expression or physical touch, confining men to an inarticulacy which is outward silence and inward deadness:

We were never able to say one truthful word to each other.
We were both more intent on holding the show of bravery
together than wanting to meet in an admission of our uncertainties and fears. That's why, today, I feel a strange, sad
sense of mutuality with him, mixed in with the occasional
spurts of anger. The mutuality comes, I think, from the way
we both denied the emotional principle in our lives.[14]

Jackson goes on to accept that his own failure to establish a
trusting and communicative relationship with his son (born of
his first marriage) is something of a legacy from his relationship with his own father. He exposes how the dysfunctions of
his own family relationships through the generations are not
only personal and specific, but represent the operation of
masculinity as a social practice.

This form of reflection on how particular masculinities
function (or dysfunction) as social practice enables men to
understand some of the complex emotional ambiguities of
their lives – it adds human 'depth' to the analysis. In his book
on father-son relationships the therapist Samuel Osherson
considers his attempts not to allow the pressures of work and
a fear of intimacy to separate him from his young son Toby. In
so doing he realizes some of the difficulties and ambivalences
which his own father must have experienced because of socially defined norms which seemed to prescribe his masculinity:

Sitting in my office one day after rushing out of the house
because of an early morning appointment, yearning still to
be in our kitchen with my new born baby and my wife, I
wondered what it was like for my father to walk to his car
every morning, beginning his long daily commute to the
Bronx, leaving a cosy breakfast scene to make his way to the
harsh public world of men. Did he feel the brief relief I did
at getting back into the safe, orderly world of work? Did he
too feel a sense of exile from a home within which he was
struggling to find a place? Much of my father's behaviour
began to make sense to me.[15]

Osherson's thesis is that men will never be able to participate in relationships as mature and communicative partners, parents or friends whilst they have within them the 'father hunger' and the memory of the 'wounded father' – the angry, sad, unloved and unloving image of masculinity, the model of manhood as control, distance, emotional silence which passes from father to son, and all too often manifests itself in violence and sexual abuse. Osherson's solution is at once both intensely personal/psychotherapeutic and radically social. Only by 'diving into the wreck of the past and retrieving a firm, sturdy appreciation of the heroism and failure in our fathers' lives' will healing come for men.[16] But this personal task is to be undertaken in the knowledge that otherwise fathers and sons are continually trapped within the social constructions of masculinity – 'captives of choices that are not satisfying to them'.[17] Men's analysis of masculinity is to bear fruit in changed practice: fatherhood becomes practical parenting, with fathers and mothers sharing in child-care. The desire for this will bring about a change in social policy to facilitate it. The personal and the political are inter-connected.

David Cohen's book *Being a Man* has a similar aim of reflecting upon his experience critically in order to expose the abusive and oppressive behavioural patterns and social stereotypes which men sustain, to their own detriment. In this book Cohen's personal experience is interwoven with the findings of psychological research and a variety of theories about masculine and feminine identity drawn from a range of disciplines. He is conscious of his debt to feminism for the understanding that 'the personal is political', but also for the conviction that there must be structural changes in the ordering of society if men and women are to enjoy relationships of equality and personal fulfilment. The agenda for change which Cohen sets out arises from his experience as a son, husband, father, worker, and 'single' man. The chapter 'Personal' tells of his relationship with Aileen, whom he meets as a student in the 1970s and marries soon after graduation. Cohen recalls that initially he was ambivalent about marriage, feeling 'caught' by Aileen, but he took pleasure in the prospect of her always loving him and supporting him, in a sense, making emotional capital out of the imbalance in their commitment. Aileen becomes pregnant; Cohen goes with her to the ante-natal classes and attends the birth of the baby, though he feels a stranger in the alien world of the delivery room and the maternity hospital. As a father he is not allowed by the medical staff to hold his new-born son for long, and when mother and baby come home from hospital he has only a day or two off work to help and be involved. As baby Nicholas grows, work remains the driving force in Cohen's life: the pressure to provide, to earn money and build a career, to perform successfully and gain a reputation, find professional satisfaction and financial security. Aileen is at home caring for Nicholas. Cohen feels unsure of his son, distant from him; this is a physical alienation as well as an emotional one, for he senses his own bigness and unfamiliarity with the tiny child, his 'clumsiness'. He is too anxious about the following day's work to get up to the crying child in the night. He is repulsed by the foul nappies. His commitments beyond the home are too much of a concern for him to notice the extent of Aileen's exhaustion with the demands of caring for and responding to Nicholas.

> Though I could accept in my head feminist arguments when Aileen was pregnant, I did nothing practical about them. Nothing I knew, had learned, or wanted to learn, suggested that a normal man had much to do with bringing up his child. I did want to be different. But not that much different.[18]

Gradually, almost despite himself and his circumstances, in response to the magical allure of the child, Cohen gains confidence with Nicholas, in touching him, playing with him, caring for him. Yet he fails to see how isolated and unhappy Aileen becomes. He relies on his wife to support him in his work, and though he puts immense effort into succeeding professionally, he does not assess how much Aileen is giving of herself in different ways to help him, whilst she receives very little emotional support in return. There is little mutuality in the relationship. Aileen's dissatisfaction pours out one

evening while they are together on holiday. Her resentment at
the situation comes as a shock to Cohen, who has been blind
to the imbalance in the relationship. He promises to 'improve'.
On their return Aileen joins a women's group, and for the first
time feels that her misery is understood. Together they experi-
ment with more mutuality in the relationship. Aileen begins to
renegotiate the marriage. She insists that David should take a
share in the domestic work and take more of a part in caring
for Nicholas. Cohen complies, with resentment, conscious that
he is working outside the home, earning the sole income.

Aileen begins to discover new confidence. She begins to
explore her sexual attraction towards women. Cohen tries
to co-operate with Aileen's process of 'finding herself', sup-
presses his anger in order, he tells himself, to carry on doing
the job he has to do. But in retrospect Cohen sees that as a man
he had learnt no appropriate ways of expressing his emotions.
There is a time when Cohen gives up work for some months
and the family goes to live in Greece, planning to earn a living
from freelance journalism and aiming to spend as much time
together as possible, with both parents having an equal share
in childcare. Cohen rejoices in the experience of being able to
participate fully in being a parent without the pressures
imposed by an employer and inflexible professional responsibilities. Yet the very status of being free from regular employment means that the income is insufficient, and the family
returns to London and a conventional routine. Though the
marriage gels for a time, and they have another son, Reuben,
the relationship is under massive strain. At the time of writing
Cohen was living near Aileen, but separately, sharing in the
care of their sons, and managing his work commitments in
order to do so responsibly.

In the course of telling his story, Cohen explores issues of
relationship, sexual identity, work and paid employment,
emotional expression, fatherhood. This exploration he undertakes in response to his encounter with feminism and the
women's movement, mindful of social and psychological
theories about masculinity, of images and stereotypes, and the
ways in which these do or do not operate in the reality of

men's lives. Cohen's conclusions are that men do value relationship, that they are concerned about women and about
their children, that they are emotional beings just as women
are, but that an overwhelming fear of powerlessness often pre-
vents men from connecting with feelings and expressing them
in any meaningful or constructive way. Men are constricted
and diminished by the ways in which work and production
are organized, which cheats them of their children and breeds
in them an insatiable desire to succeed and a crippling fear of
failure. Yet men collude with these systems as almost the only
way they know of 'being a man'. Cohen's own experience is
that although he was able to make an intellectual assent to the
needs and assertions of his partner, in practice he did not
undertake all the emotional and practical work which was
required of him to secure a mutually fulfilling relationship.
The challenges of his relationship with Aileen undermined his
sense of who he was as a man:

> The situations I've described were confusing and emotional
> enough. But for me, they were also fraught because I was
> being made to feel things that were not really 'appropriate'
> to a man. We are schooled to success – not to feel pain,
> abandonment, betrayal.[19]

Given the constraints of masculinity which Cohen
describes, perhaps what is extraordinary is that he is able to
articulate the range of experiences which he does so publicly
and with such candour, and this seems true for David Jackson
too. What is significant is that these men have identified their
own fear of powerlessness and have been able to allow themselves to become vulnerable enough to express this to others –
not least to other men. This would seem to be an important
gesture in response to the feminist critique of patriarchal
power as these men have encountered it in their own experience. Cohen believes that men *do* want to change, and are
changing, in order to be more responsive partners and lovers,
more involved fathers. Yet the demands and prospect and
processes of this change are painful and difficult, not least

because the way men are men is as much a matter of social organization as personal inclination.

Though feminism has created this demand for change, and women often initiate it in men through change in their own lives, it is something which many men want for themselves. Cohen's feeling is that women should do more to 'reach out' towards men and help them learn new ways of being men. Women and men together should make the organization of work a matter for urgent political consideration and change if men and women are to have a more equal share in the care of children, more equal power in society, and more satisfying emotional relationships and sexual partnerships. Even writers who have a deep antipathy to feminism, as Neil Lyndon professes to have in his polemical *No More Sex War*, seek a new formula for men and women to share equitably the work and reward of bringing up children. Lyndon believes that beyond the anger and resentment men feel because of the way feminism has misrepresented them, fathers are longing to participate in the love and nurture of their children from which they have been so long excluded. Lyndon is less candid about how this exclusion operates, and the extent to which men have, wittingly or unwittingly, excluded themselves.

Autobiography, especially where it is undertaken with a critical awareness of gender, leads into an agenda for social change. This is particularly the case in the realms of paternity and employment. Yet the agenda being set is that of professional men. How changing work patterns and mass unemployment are affecting men in general, and issues of male crime, violence, drug addiction among young men who are socially and economically disfranchised, and the whole area of men's responsibility for 'unfathered' or abandoned children, are largely unaddressed in these texts.

Changing men

It would seem that the language and emphasis of the men's movement as characterized by the mythopoeic writers is the subject of much negative criticism from feminist thinkers, who see its particular focus on the psychological needs of men as exclusivist. The essentialist approach is interpreted as something of a collusion with the existing pattern of relations between women and men, including its all-pervasive male domination and systemic violence. This line of interpretation is too crude. The writings of Bly do not endorse violence, but they do fail to make clear the nature of the Wild Man and associated archetypes in a context where violence against women, together with economic and sexual exploitation, is being perpetrated by men. The essentialist aim is to work towards a balance in gender relations for which men must be newly equipped by a transformed self-understanding. Integral to this vision of a renewed masculinity is a movement away from those aspects of conventional male roles and self-understanding which have proven harmful to men, including those aspects which have hampered men's relationships with women and children. The aim is to offer a vision of a culture which affirms men and empowers them to live a masculinity which is not grounded in isolation and a terror of intimacy: an alternative to the present culture which inducts men into violence, addiction or emotional numbness.

But essentialist writers are responding to men's anger, confusion and dismay without helping men to acknowledge in any significant way feminism's critique of men's power. The mythopoeic emphasis is therapeutic: a response to men's 'grief' in a culture which has been emasculated. Yet this therapy is hampered if it is blind to the reality of male power. It would seem to lack the reciprocity of men's self-examination which the constructionist approaches have, characterized by the theory of gender relations. Connell sees the 'masculinity therapy' of Bly and his like as limited in its concerns and reactionary in its implications – 'an adaption of patriarchal structures through the *modernization* of masculinity', merely working to bring about an 'accommodation between men and women, adjustment at the level of personal relations' rather than a far-reaching cultural shift.[20]

Yet, as many constructionist writers acknowledge, it is in the realm of the personal and the inter-personal that men are feeling the need for transformation. Though the writings of Bly and Keen and their like have been dismissed by constructionist writers such as Connell, the Jungian psychology of these books, and the workshops and therapeutic groups accompanying them, have captured men's imaginations in a way which the rather academical tone of much of the constructionist literature has yet to do. It may well be that the mythopoeic approach offers men a soothing balm for egos bruised by feminism whilst deflecting them from the more serious and crucial analysis of their participation within the lived structures of men's power over women. But the significance of their appeal to the *imaginative* in men should not be discounted, nor should the connections which are made between the spiritual, emotional, sexual and psychological aspects of masculinity as men test out replacements for the worn cultural images of manhood. The essentialist appeal for men may be its capacity to offer dynamic new ideals, images and heroes; its engagement with fantasy, the emotions and with experience of the spiritual may be more compelling for men than the language of theory. The latter has a controlled reasonableness and definiteness which may seem all too familiar male. The ideas of Bly, and even more so those of Keen, connect the social and personal with the ecological. Their talk of 'wilderness' is compelling for men who feel themselves to be alienated from the 'natural' world as well as from women and their own 'true' identity as men. These are philosophies for an era of ecological consciousness.

Yet much of the constructionist work on men and masculinity arises out of men's groups and, significantly, out of conversation with women (predominantly in the academic sphere). The social agendas arising out of critical autobiography, and the implications for practical change which men's groups and 'hands on' publications such as *Achilles Heel* engender, show that the theorization of masculinity as an aspect of gender relations goes hand in hand with its transformation.

However, as Connell points out, in comparison with the gay movement the 'project of transforming masculinity' manifests very little life or influence among men in general, who are supposed to be its constituency.[21] This comment applies to the whole range of approaches which are reconsidering masculinity. Even so, they are significant. For in Connell's assessment, what characterizes these various enterprises around masculinity is that they all 'accept the fact of social transformations of masculinity'; in their diversity, each manifests the 'consciousness of historical change in gender'.[22] It is in this sense that the metaphors of *constructing* masculinity and *journeying* towards masculinity (even towards regaining a lost, essential masculinity) are aspects of an inter-connected awakening, re-imagining and re-construction of masculinity which is both personal and social, psychological and physical, spiritual and political – a multiplicity of inter-relations.

It would be doing violence to the diversity in the study of men and masculinity to attempt to fuse what is distinct, but both constructionist and essentialist approaches articulate a sense of crisis among men in Western culture. Both envisage this crisis as a positive opportunity for men. Writers from both perspectives have articulated a sense of anger in men who have felt themselves to be misrepresented, or even in some cases degraded, by the critiques of feminism and their experience of the women's movement. Yet none characterize themselves as misogynist or anti-women. Some are firmly allied to the women's movement and acknowledge their ideological debt to feminism. Others acknowledge the importance of feminism in contending its ideas. As a whole, the writing is articulating men's uncertainty on social and theoretical levels, and in the areas of personal identity and relationship. This is being interpreted as the signal for initiating new ways of conceptualizing and living out the masculine.

What has opened up through these studies of masculinity is an exploration of the areas of men's lives which are causing them pain. Men are beginning to articulate needs which arise from the present ways of being men, and these felt needs are pointing towards the possibilities of change and growth. Men are seeking to foster more emotional self-awareness, and to nurture free and constructive ways of expressing feelings which do not employ verbal, physical or sexual violence. There is a desire to develop amongst men the capacity for closer relationships with one another and to tackle the fears associated with male intimacy. Men are lamenting the breakdown in father-son relationships, and are looking for ways to heal those relationships and to provide social and personal ways for men to be more nurturing and involved fathers to their own children. Men are seeking an integrated sense of self which does not objectify the body; men are beginning to be excited by the variety and complexity of sexual desire, wanting to be more communicative, less performing partners for their lovers and wives. Men are acknowledging the competitivism and achievement-orientated values which motivate their relationships and work patterns, and the physical and emotional damage that this is doing.

The pursuit of justice

Bob Connell's doubts about 'masculinity therapy' are well placed in so far as they draw attention to the dangers of men transforming masculinity in order to maintain something approximating the existing order in gender relations. Masculinities may be adjusted, but men's advantage over women may remain unchanged.[23] The real issue, Connell argues, is where difference in gender becomes the ground for domination and disadvantage – whether in terms of inequality of pay, boys being given more food than girls, the interruption of women's speech in conversation, or violence against gays as 'feminized men'. He suggests (imagines?) a programme of 'de-gendering' and 're-gendering' which would be part of a new 'gender multiculturism' where difference is celebrated rather than exploited, and in which women and men, gay and straight, would freely participate in a range of social activity unhindered by the present boundaries of gender. Men would experience a 'reimbodiment' as they change nappies, play with children, clean up messes and care for the old. Building on gay and feminist ideas of utopia, Connell's programme is one of reconfiguration and recomposition, to 'combine symbolically gendered activities: body-builders can work in kindergartens, lesbians can wear leather jackets, boys can learn to cook'.[24]

Connell might have added that women can be deacons, priests and bishops, and that gay men can participate in the church crêche whilst lesbians serve coffee and straight men take their turn on the flower rota. It is where men's social practice changes in alliance with women that transformation in masculinity is most likely to occur, rather than through a 'men's movement', Connell suggests. He regards social justice in gender relations as a matter of men working against their own interests, a cause which, in his view, is unlikely to inspire mass solidarity among men. But where issues of gender arise in contexts other than those of 'pure gender politics', situations where 'solidarity among men is pursued for reasons other than masculinity', then that solidarity 'may support a project of gender justice, especially where there is explicit solidarity with women in the same situation'.[25] Connell cites labour and socialist politics, anti-colonial resistance movements, movements for cultural democracy and racial equality as examples of this 'alliance politics' among men and women. If such politics can be extended to include people of different ages, sexual orientations, races and social classes, as Connell's vision of gender multiculturalism suggests, then this social programme begs questions of the community of the church. Can the social practice of *koinonia* within the church embrace gender multiculturalism? Will the transformation of masculinity within the Christian community only come about as women, black people and gay people are empowered? Are men within the church able to see their 'loss of power' to groups which challenge patriarchal domination as an opportunity to create new forms of manhood which can contribute to the alliance politics of the community?

Where the theology of churches inspires them to be communities which embrace all people, men are able to share in a moment of opportunity. Their experience of leadership exercised by women, for example, or of feminine language for the divine and feminist-inspired liturgies, may offer men a new experience of themselves as men, and changed understandings of what masculinity may be about.

As we have seen, Elaine Graham suggests that an awareness of the critical theory of gender implies that all Christian theology and practice is gendered – and therefore is relational and provisional.[26] Such an awareness on the part of men could be an encouragement to share in a project of re-gendering the church in ways that are more just. Men, women, gay people and black people could participate together in reconfiguring the practice and theology of the Christian community, rather than lapsing into a reactionary defence of 'tradition', or negating all creative enterprise to those who are reforging the churches from their marginalized position within them or beyond them. Of course, the experience of the Christian community to date shows how powerful the forces for change can be, and how entrenched the defence of patriarchy – in short, how difficult alliance politics can be where men are confronted with the loss of power, and when their own complex masculinities are dangerously challenged.

The ordination of women and the (homo)sexuality debates within the Church of England are two examples where the 'myth of masculinity' – that men have an homogenous identity corporately and personally – has been challenged. The ordination of women not only challenges male authority by incorporating women into leadership roles, thereby opening up the church for transformation. In addition, for some men it endangers their capacity to 'become feminine', to show care, intimacy and vulnerability, whilst retaining an identity which is exclusively, if ambiguously, male: that of the priest. The ordination of women as priests compromises this careful ambiguity in masculine identity and function. In a connected way, the recognition of homosexuality within the Christian community is not only a challenge to the predominance of male heterosexuality in shaping the ethics and pastoral practice of the churches. It also questions the assumptions about sexual desire which are part of conventional masculinity, revealing that men's sexuality is far more diverse, complex and fluid than patriarchal models would allow.

Both these issues continue to cause pain and turmoil within the churches, whilst women and gays are seen as interlopers and transgressors of the church's unity and holiness. But some insights of men's reflexivity would suggest that the real obstacle to fellowship is men's persistence with models of masculinity which deny the realities of male sexual desire and base men's identity upon the patriarchal domination of 'the other'. What is at risk for men is nothing more and nothing less than the collapse of a patriarchal tradition which, in men's lived experience, is neither healthy, satisfying nor integrated. But the familiar flesh-pots of Egypt are more comfortable than the difficult journey through a strange country, and Connell's enthusiasm for men's reimbodiment through practical care entails back-breaking work which most would avoid if possible! Yet the task for masculine theology is to reach beyond anger and fear and point towards a masculinity which is appropriate for a world framed by feminism and gay sexuality and the developing ecological consciousness and partnership of world faiths and ethical stances. The task for men is to learn how to co-operate, to develop masculinities which may fully and fruitfully participate in the ongoing creation and recreation of human and ecological community where diversity is celebrated. Such a project might seem far from orthodox Christianity, and yet the pursuit of harmony and peace is one which lies at the heart of the Christian vision and practice, the sustaining of an earthly community which mirrors the divine life: a 'sociality of harmonious difference'.[27]

6

Behold the Man: The Jesuses of Masculine Theology

When I was a child, one of my great pleasures was to read Ladybird books. I would be captivated by the wonderful conjunction of simple, informative text and on the opposite page a picture full of colourful, bold images. Among my favourite Ladybirds was the one about English cathedrals: I loved to study the lines of the soaring arches and enormous pillars, the pictures of Salisbury's spire, York's rose window, the ascending grandeur of Canterbury's interior. Towards the end of the book were pictures of the modern buildings: Liverpool's Metropolitan Cathedral, and of course, Coventry. I remember the illustration of Coventry very clearly – a coloured drawing of the wide open interior of the nave which was so different from the others, drawing the eye up to the strangely angular shower of shapes above the stalls in the choir, and beyond to the vast image of the tapestry on the east wall above the altar, the seated figure in white with powerful face and hands, and a tiny figure beneath, standing between the flesh of bare feet.

I cannot exactly remember the text which accompanied this drawing, and it was only much later when I visited the cathedral as an adult that I realized I had misinterpreted what must have been written there. It may be that I was given the book before I could read very well, or perhaps it is just that I paid very little attention to the words, but I formed the powerful and definite impression that the immense tapestry of Coventry was depicting the figure of a woman. I supposed her to be Mary the mother of Jesus. To my eyes the shape of the seated figure depicted in the book was a woman's shape: she had wide hips, full breasts, rounded thighs. She was wearing a dress. Her white costume was a puzzling kind of gown, low cut around the neck and blooming from the waist downwards – almost the kind of garment worn by the aristocratic women in historical and fairy-tale Ladybird books. The big figure at the end of Coventry Cathedral was definitely a woman, definitely Mary, and the tiny figure between her feet was Jesus, nestled like a shy and uncertain toddler wanting to shelter with his mother from the stranger who is busy gazing at him.

Though I know now that Sutherland's great image which presides over the building is an image of Jesus Christ, and have seen the tapestry in its full, real-life splendour, and have studied the face to see that it is bearded, and the neck and the shoulders and the large hands to see that they are those of a man, what persists in my mind's eye is the perception of a female figure. What I still see from a distance is a tapestry woman – an almost uterine shape in abstract, the form of a plump, perhaps even pregnant woman – a powerful, swollen female. What I see when I come much closer is what I know rationally to be the case: the tapestry depicts the figure of a man. Yet the other impression still has its pull. When I focus on the beard and the heavy shoulders what I see is a man who is dressed in the clothes of a woman, a kind of Jesus in drag, a pantomime dame, a man who has clumsily assumed his idea of a feminine appearance. He is trying to mother this figure between his feet. For all his bigness and physical power, he is trying to be gentle with this lonely, rather tortured, defiant individual, who is so much smaller than himself.

Coventry's Christ is for me a sexually ambivalent figure, part man, part woman. He is a bearded woman-Christ. She is a Christ-like fulsome woman, a fertility goddess. What I see is a depiction of Christ which subverts, contravenes, questions his maleness, presenting an ambiguous masculinity; one which strangely suggests his femininity, and in so doing at the same time re-emphasizes his maleness and redefines it. What I take from the tapestry is an impression of a dissident Christ, a figure which confuses gender whilst asserting it in all its fixedness and fluidity.

What Daphne Hampson sees in the tapestry is very different.[1] She is more definite about what she sees: a figuration of Christ in glory which represents an illustration of patriarchal religion, a display of male-devised Christianity in which domination is divinized. The great male God-figure of Jesus towers massively above the tiny human being at his feet. Power, enlightenment, autonomy, understanding, all these are vested in the larger, dominant figure. The human being is depicted as being dependent upon power beyond herself and her control, located in the divine realm of a 'personal', 'realist' God rather than within the personhood of the human individual and the sociality of human community. In Hampson's view, the tapestry is very much a visual celebration of patriarchy schematized in the symbolic relationship of the enormous man-God Jesus Christ and the shrunken human form beneath him.

In this viewing of the tapestry, Christ's masculinity is not so much a matter of physical detail; his maleness is an aspect of his relationship with the tiny human form. It is the massiveness and domination of the Christ figure in relation to 'the other' beneath him which manifests his maleness.

Whether in the schemes of art, spiritual devotion or theology, the figure of Jesus Christ may have different meanings and different effects upon those who encounter him. In particular, the man Jesus becomes the bearer of differing masculinities. Christ is fashioned and re-fashioned as the example which the faithful are to imitate, but as a purely male example he becomes the role-model for men as men. In taking Jesus as an archetype of masculinity Sam Keen finds in him the perfection of a manhood defined in 'relational terms', a virility which is found in communion with God and others, a masculinity practised in a life of compassion and self-surrender. Keen is clear that masculinity is a product of history and culture given expression in the ongoing process of re-interpreting the Jesus figure:

Discussions about manhood in Western culture cannot avoid the figure of Jesus. He is the most frequently used mirror in which generations of Western men – philosophers from Augustine to Tillich, evangelists from Paul to Billy Graham, novelists from Renan to Kazantzakis – have seen their own faces reflected. Like the ink blots used in the psychological Rorschach test, Jesus is the historical X on which men project their own self-understanding. Every generation discovers a different Jesus – the magical saviour, the wonder worker, the mystic, the political rebel, the labour organizer, the capitalist, the communist, the greatest salesman who ever lived, the protofeminist, the ecologist. As Albert Schweitzer said, men searching for the historical Jesus look into a deep, dark well, see a reflection of themselves, and call it 'Lord'.[2]

Most contemporary literature on men and masculinity does not share Keen's sense of Jesus as the primary 'bearer' of masculinity in our present culture. Jesus is no longer *the* man. However, for the theological reflections on masculinity which have begun to develop in response to feminist theology, the masculinity of Jesus Christ remains significant and formative. Some feminist theology has focussed on the maleness of the Saviour as a problem within a broader critical theology of Christianity under patriarchy.[3] Such theologies have questioned whether a male saviour may be a saviour for women who are oppressed by men, and theologies and iconographies of the *Christa* have developed in which the humanity of the Saviour figure is given an emphasis by presenting the Christ as woman. In contrast, the theologies of masculinity, all written by men, assume the maleness of Christ to be unproblematical in soteriological terms. Yet in the current climate of gender-consciousness, theologies which centre on the significance of Christ's masculinity also raise the issue of femininity. The gender of Christ becomes a focus for exploring the relationship between male and female, masculine and feminine.

Furthermore, the masculinity of Jesus accrues new value and takes on a soteriological significance. In these theologies Jesus Christ is invested as the exemplar of masculinity for a culture in which feminism is an influential force. Jesus is inter-

preted and promoted as *the* man by male theologians writing
in a consciously gendered world. Jesus Christ becomes an icon
in gender theology. He is a representative man in whom men
find judgment and challenge as men. He is a man in whom
men find inspiration and affirmation for their belief and
practice as men. The theological significance of Jesus is being
interpreted in relation to many of the concerns of men which
have found expression in the literature of men's studies. Jesus
becomes a model for men's relations with women; he is understood to embody a male sexuality and a male intimacy which
is perfect; in him the fractured relationship between the body
and spirit, the mind and emotions, is healed; as Son of the
Father he lives in the ideal father-son relationship; in Jesus
men may find a new model for friendship. In addition to these
concerns, the masculinity of Jesus Christ has taken on
significance in terms of mission, evangelism and pastoral care
for men, and new models of ministry and discipleship have
been built around the kinds and modes of masculinity which
Jesus is understood to embody and practice. The masculinity
of Jesus has assumed a new theological significance for men
who are articulating a dis-ease with the conventions of manhood, and also for men who are seeking to defend or renew a
masculinity 'in crisis'. As Garrison Keillor says in *The Book of
Guys*: 'guys are in trouble … guys are gloomy … Years ago,
manhood was an opportunity for achievement, and now it is a
problem to be overcome.'[4] For some, Jesus the man offers a
solution for troubled men. But the masculinities of Jesus are
multifarious and conflicting.

Jesus as archetype

Jungian writers such as Robert Moore and Douglas Gillette
write from their clinical experience as therapists, which
suggests to them that 'something vital is missing in the inner
lives of many of the men who seek psychotherapy', and that
this deficiency is not an inadequate connection with the 'inner
feminine', but an alienation from the 'deep and instinctual
masculine energies, the potentials of mature masculinity'.[5] Bly

suggests in *Iron John* that men are suffering from the absence of ritual processes in Western culture whereby boys may be initiated into mature manhood. Patriarchy is the expression of this immature masculinity, a cultural and social structure which 'expresses stunted masculinity, fixated at immature levels', and as such imposes conventions and stereotypes which damage men as well as women. Patriarchy thus disables 'true' masculinity as well as 'true' femininity, and men must find ways to access for themselves the energies of mature masculinity as they present themselves in the masculine archetypes such as those of King, Warrior, Magician, Lover.

In his exploration of the relation of sexuality and gender to spirituality, Patrick Arnold sets out to describe the unique qualities of a specifically masculine spirituality through the concept of archetypal psychology. His book *Wildmen, Warriors, and Kings* interprets principal male figures in the scriptures as revealers of the classical masculine archetypes: Abraham is the Patriarch and Pilgrim, Moses the Warrior and Magician, Solomon the King, Elijah the Wildman, Elisha the Healer, Jeremiah the Prophet, Jonah the Trickster, and David, Jonathan and Solomon are examples of the Lover figure. Each of these archetypes is nuanced: it has its shadow side, and it is manifested in a variety of ways in different personalities, and can be seen to be active and energizing in the lives of holy men through history as they are true to the call and pattern which arises within themselves. St Francis of Assisi is a Wildman, Martin Luther King a Magic Warrior. Arnold explores four of these archetypes – Wildman, Warrior, King, and Father – as metaphors for the divine, and goes on to suggest that these essentially masculine metaphors offer an insight into the nature and experience of the unknowable God. Thus God's 'love of life', his power, freedom, justice, love and care, these are all essentially masculine qualities, and so what we know of God through revelation might be described as his masculinity, and should be celebrated as such.[6]

Within this scheme Jesus of Nazareth is the Christ archetype – a 'spiritual quality' which 'surfaces so magnificently in the person of the historical Jesus'.[7] The qualities of the Christ

archetype are detachment, redemptive suffering and inde-
structibility, qualities which might also be recognized in the
lives of the Buddha, Gandhi and Nelson Mandela. But in
Arnold's view the Gospels portray Jesus in terms of all the
classical male archetypes to reveal him as 'the ultimate spiritual archetype'. Jesus is King in his 'quality of soul', 'internal
nobility' and 'psychic greatness'; he is Warrior in his fight
against hypocrisy, lies and injustice, and in his final heroic
self-sacrifice; he is Trickster and Fool in his wit and sub-
versiveness, and ultimately in the folly of the cross. Jesus is the
'fulfilment of masculinity' and the 'goal of mature manhood',
and by following Jesus a man is initiated into 'Christhood',
and in taking Jesus as his model, in 'activating his Christ
potential', a man 'participates in the very life of God, becoming his adopted son'.[8]

Given his enthusiasm for all this divinely manifested
masculinity, Arnold attempts to demonstrate that in becoming
the man Jesus, God does not prioritize the male over the
female, and stresses that the 'Christ-self' may be assumed by
women as well as men (for example Catherine of Siena and
Mother Teresa of Calcutta). In Arnold's view, the incarnation
of God as a man reveals a kind of divine gender bias, for the
revelation of God in Jesus the Christ (if this is what the revelation of the Christ archetype in Jesus means!) shows the extent
of God's salvation in reaching even the most needy, for 'the
divine epiphany of the Christ in a historical male is, if anything, an act of divine compassion and outreach to help the
most vulnerable human beings – men – on their way to God'.[9]

Jesus as embodiment of masculine wholeness

In his essay 'On Men's Liberation', James Nelson is explicit in
his recognition that any critical attention men may pay to
themselves as men is a result of the women's movement, a
response to the feelings of 'confusion, frustration and anger'
which arise in men who are challenged to change by feminism[10] – a point we have encountered elsewhere. In looking
back over his development and life as boy and man, Nelson

gives voice to a radical dissatisfaction. In acknowledging what
women suffer as a result of male domination, Nelson begins to
recognize that men also suffer. They do not suffer to the extent
that women do, or in the same ways, but men's alienation
from their bodies and emotions, their lack of intimacy with
one another, their fear of homosexuality, their estrangement
from their fathers, their obsessive competitivism – these are
real issues for men which distort them as human persons and
distort social institutions.

Nelson finds the theological solution for this alienation of
men from themselves and one another in the gospel of love, in
the message 'You are accepted', in the love which casts out the
fear he sees at the root of all sexism and prejudice. In the
gospel men who are afraid may find assurance, an assurance
for their fears of not meeting the father-God's expectations.
This gospel speaks directly to men's fear of failure, emotions,
impotence and loss of control. Men need to know that they are
fully and unconditionally loved by God in Christ, and that this
love gives them worth which cannot be won or earned but is
inalienable and therefore need not be defended from failure
sexually, professionally or socially. Human being has been
graced in the incarnation, and it is in a spirituality grounded
in the body, in physical and sexual experience, that men are to
receive a new vision of themselves. Jesus Christ becomes the
model for men who are seeking release from the prison of conventional masculinity:

> Am I afraid of losing my power and control? If so, there is
> that paradoxical figure who counted equality with God not
> a thing to be grasped, but emptied himself. He is the one
> who washed the disciples' feet.
> Am I afraid of losing my strong, masculine, heterosexual
> image? Am I afraid of vulnerability and intimacy? If so, I
> need to look again at the man who wept, who embraced the
> beloved disciple, who called out to others in his time of
> need.[11]

Nelson is very clear that what is crucial in incarnational

theology is the humanity of Jesus rather than his maleness.[12] Yet the maleness of Jesus is an integral part of his humanity, and Nelson finds in Jesus the man a 'compelling picture of male sexual wholeness, of creative masculinity, and of the redemption of manhood from both oppresiveness and superficiality', for in Jesus men may 'find clues ... toward a richer and more authentic masculinity'.[13]

This is not Jesus as the church conventionally presents him, a man without sexuality, one who is hardly a bodily being. This is Jesus as the artists of the Renaissance represented him, a Jesus who is fully human, fully physical, fully male. Nelson draws on the work of Leo Steinberg's *The Sexuality of Christ in Renaissance Art and in Modern Oblivion* to show how the philosophy of the Renaissance allowed a rediscovery of Christ's bodiliness, given its fullest expression in the portrayal of Christ's genitals in art. For men who are alienated from their physicality and sexuality, this sexual Jesus can be an icon of a redeemed maleness.

Nelson sets out to follow the pattern set by feminist theologians in doing 'body theology' for men, a theology which is rooted in the male physical and sexual experience. He finds a spiritual meaning in the male genitals. The two modes of men's genital experience – the erect phallus and the flaccid penis – are modes of revelation for men.[14] In the power and hardness of their erect penis men may find the physical embodiment of strength, assertiveness, determination, the spirituality of the *via positiva*. Yet in the softness and vulnerability of the flaccid penis men find their gentleness and passivity, a capacity for nurture, an undemanding and relaxed way of being, a stillness, darkness and waiting, the spirituality of the *via negativa*. If men would accept their bodies and their sexualities as God-given and as part of the goodness of human being then they would begin to understand the complex integrity of sexual-spiritual self, and they would come to know that these experiences of the erect and flaccid penis are both profoundly masculine. They represent a complementarity in men which, once acknowledged, takes them beyond the androgynous ideal. For androgyny implies that a man must develop *feminine* qualities in order to be nurturing, receptive and passive. But a man's genital experiences, men's 'bilingual bodies', suggest both power and softness, passivity and action, a 'marvellous conjunction of apparent opposites in the male's sexual body … a wholeness inviting him to richness of personhood'.[15] What men must seek is masculine fullness rather than their 'feminine side', a notion which seems to imply the importing of alien qualities to deficient men. Men have an integrity which is intrinsically theirs, but one which is lost in their fears of intimacy and physicality and vulnerability. Through a sexual theology of what it means to be a man, men may recover their fullness as masculine human beings, and such fullness will not be based on 'unilateral power' which seeks independence and self-sufficiency, but on 'relational power', power which is shared and interdependent and mutual. For in their genital experience men may come to know the reciprocity of their sexual power – that both the phallus and the penis have affect and are affected, and that a man's sexual experience involves both 'making claims and absorbing influence'.[16]

Nelson believes that the Jesus of Renaissance art is Jesus represented as truly human, as a sexual male human being, and so represented he offers men a positive image of masculinity, an embodiment of maleness which does not define itself in negative terms (not woman, not gay, not vulnerable, not needing), but one which is a sexual spiritual wholeness. For Jesus is a man in whom the 'intimate connection' between the sexual and the spiritual is intact, and as such he is the revealer of what men are intended by God to be, the 'teacher, embodiment, and releaser of relational power – a judgment on our phallic unilateral power, but also an invitation to a full-bodied life-giving mutuality'.[17] And what Jesus' male humanity, perfectly attuned to God's power and grace as it was, offers all human beings is the 'Christic reality', the embracing of the divine life in all that which makes us more truly human.[18]

Jesus as relational hero

In his book *Men and Masculinity: From Power to Love*, Roy McCloughry draws attention to familiar issues which are the concerns of men's studies – the difficulties men have in identifying their needs and acknowledging their fears, particularly the fear of women, together with the issues relating to men and fatherhood, sexuality, intimacy, self-expression, work and worklessness. For men who acknowledge these issues, Jesus may be both hero and mentor.[19] He is a model to emulate, a leader to follow, indeed, he is the ultimate human being – one able to attract both women and men in that his humanity combines 'all the desirable characteristics of men and women ... capable of expressing anger but very nurturing. Strong in a crisis yet also vulnerable'.[20] Though divine, Jesus is truly human, a hero who identifies with women and men as they are, and in following Jesus people may become more and more like him – the perfect human being – and so more and more they become their true selves.[21] But this Jesus is more than a theological symbol. His incarnation is divine love in practice. As a man of his time Jesus subverts masculine power in the way he acts and relates, particularly in his attitude and behaviour towards women. Unlike the men of his day, he accepted the touch of women and conversed with them. He showed a new way of being and a new form of power – the power of love – in laying aside the privilege of divinity and assuming the form of a servant. The incarnation of God in a man who subverts the conventions of patriarchal power makes Jesus the hero for a time when men's power is exposed as exploitative of women and damaging to men. This Jesus reveals to men a new way of being male. He is 'of the male sex but not the masculine gender', he 'does not wear the masks of masculinity as men since him have done', nor does he 'have a division between his inner self and his outer image', nor was he 'trying to prove himself a successful man according to the criteria of his day'. He is a man who is fully human in his service, love, strength, humility and intimacy. McCloughry's Jesus 'subverts masculinity and in doing so puts flesh on the

idea of giving up power in order to be whole'.[22] As the perfect
expression of God's will for humanity, he is the norm in whom
all others, women and men together, can find true humanity –
and this is of particular hope for men, for Jesus 'must give us
hope that being a man is a sufficient basis for displaying
everything that is associated with being human'.[23]

Although his portrayal is diminished by the sexism of the
church, it is in this ultimate God-incarnate hero and no other
that men may find the pattern and power for renewal. This
pattern is corporate as well as individual. The liturgy, leadership, ministry and decision-making processes of the church
must reflect this kenosis of God in Christ, ceasing to institu-
tionalize conventional masculinity in its common life, but
following Christ and embracing the (frightening and painful)
changes involved in giving full and equal status to women
and men. This is an evangelical imperative for the Christian
community where men are conspicuous by their absence –

> If the church is to reach men, as it can and must, then it must
> confront the issue of masculinity. For it is this that is blight-
> ing men in our culture ... the Church is giving the impres-
> sion that it is underwriting masculinity (as presently consti-
> tuted), whereas what men need to see in the Church is the
> movement from power to love.[24]

Changing men, transforming community

If we begin to read contemporary theology as gendered, then
we begin to understand that the interpretation and representation of the masculinity of Jesus Christ is a recurrent symbol for
new self-understanding amongst men. Jesus is a powerful
representative for shifting notions of ideal manhood, a sign of
hope displaying the person whom all men may become in
seeking to imitate him. He is presented as a model man, *the*
man.

For Arnold, Jesus is the truly masculine man because his life
and death is wholly and actively in harmony with the essential masculine qualities inherent in all men. In this sense Jesus
is the true man's man, the paragon of maleness. For Nelson,

Jesus is the man in whom the sexual and bodily are in unity with the emotional, rational and spiritual in a divinely blessed completeness. Jesus is the embodiment of masculine wholeness – the man of integrity, the man in whom all men can see their own sexuality embodied and challenged, a vision of who they might be. The sexual man Jesus is one for whom power is not a mode of domination over women and 'weaker' men, but an opportunity for reciprocity and mutuality, a man in whom men see the possibility of their release from the prisons of fear and denial which conventional masculinity imposes. For McCloughry, Jesus is an ethical figure, a man in whom the values of justice and community find fulfilment through relationships of intimacy and respect. Jesus embodies and enacts God's forgiveness and love for a broken world in a pattern which the church must seek to emulate, a pattern which is a new kind of masculinity, and one which promises a radically transformed and transformative masculinity for all men.

To focus in this way on the masculinity of Jesus has its dangers. It is in the archetypal manhood of Jesus that these dangers are clearest. To portray Jesus as Wildman and Warrior seems to endorse the very qualities of violence and aggression which terrorize women and many men, which women have exposed and challenged and which men are questioning for themselves. In idealizing the manhood of Jesus there is a risk that Jesus is used as a kind of encouragement for men to remain unchanged in a time of radical challenge to their subordinating power; Jesus as a boost to wilting male certainties. Such a (mis)apprehension of the person and mission of Jesus Christ in terms of conventional masculine stereotypes so emphasizes the maleness of Jesus that salvation itself comes to seem a masculine project, accomplished by a man who reveals in his particular masculinity a God who is likewise masculine. Within this scheme women barely have a place. It is a spirituality of reaction to feminism and to the challenges which feminism poses to male supremacy in theology and the community of the church. It is a theology which lacks an analysis of male power and of its implications for human relationships under God.

Yet any theology which places emphasis on the masculinity of Jesus Christ takes risks with the doctrine of the incarnation in seeming to portray Christ as the exclusive Saviour of the male species because the eternal Word is incarnate in a male human being. Though Arnold stresses that the 'Christic reality' which the historical Jesus exemplifies is for women and men, the nature of Arnold's Jesus is such that he is a man in patriarchal mode, a stumbling block for women and men alike. Yet the maleness of Jesus is an historical/textual fact, and gender-consciousness must take account of this crucial aspect of his humanness.

Women theologians have made differing responses to the maleness of Jesus Christ, and some have found in it a positive significance within the divine economy, an integral part of salvation which is for all and extends to all. McCloughry quotes Diane Tennis' sense of the value of Jesus' maleness:

> Unlike women, he did not have to be a servant. He had power and access to power … (he) modelled in his own being a dramatic assault on male privilege. Who but a man could credibly teach and model such a revolution in relationships by giving up power? Only a man could do that, because only men had power.[25]

As Angela West has shown, in the incarnation of God as a man there is a particular expression of divine love and enactment of divine power; for in the betrayal, rejection, beatings, mockings and crucifixion of Jesus Christ, male power – ultimate power – was laid aside: in the man Jesus on the cross 'God denies the godhead as patriarchal power, and reveals Godself in humanity, in the helpless infant, in the helpless crucified being'.[26] Men and women do not worship the triumph of male power in Jesus, but a God who opens up a broader, richer reality than male supremacy offers.

Though the masculinities of Jesus which Arnold, Nelson and McCloughry present may inspire men toward a renewed masculinity, for Nelson and McCloughry the pattern of those masculinities implies a transformation of the power relations between men and women – the coming of gender justice and a renewed community of women and men. In Nelson's understanding, Jesus is the human who represents in his living and his dying, in his relationship with God and his love of neighbour, the incarnation of God in human lives which all may experience – a divinity which all men and women enflesh in their bodies. For McCloughry, the man Jesus models a perfect humanity which is beyond gender – he restores 'God's initial vision of a shared humanity in which men and women share in a common humanity'.[27] For Brian Wren, the masculinity of Jesus the servant, who calls his disciples (both women and men) friends, subverts the power of patriarchy. Jesus is a 'male for others', and his relationship with Abba-God manifests God's nature of love, mercy, justice, humility in a way which sets him free from patriarchy and, through the Spirit, empowers all men and women to do likewise. For Wren, the loving and liberating man Jesus overturns the old order of alienation and domination, and 'stands between God and humankind not as a wall, but as a bridge': the incarnation is 'open ended',[28] both inaugurating and sustaining a new world order where women and men are equal and free.

This is a world James Whitehead longs for when he reflects with Evelyn his wife on the practice of his relationships and ministry as a man. He sees his whole life characterized by the destructive masculine virtues of isolation and control. Men's obsession with control has been divinized in the theology of God's impassibility, and in turn this distant God becomes a model for pastors who pursue a theology of care which is 'not so much a theology as it is a masculine fantasy: to reach out in care and control while remaining untouched by others'.[29] The Whiteheads call for a 're-imagining of the masculine' which is individual and corporate, for 'images to replace our manly reserve with a passionate attachment in faith and love'.[30] They see in the scriptural image of *koinonia* (Acts 2.42) a community of partnership and mutuality which is free from domination. Where the church takes *koinonia* as its pattern men will find new modes and meanings for masculinity: it represents a theology and practice which pursues gender justice. The early

Christian community is a 'metaphor of common life' for the present. For Nelson, McCloughry and Wren, this new community begins in the masculinity of Jesus Christ.

7

Imagining Ways of Being Together

Let my soul praise you that it may love you, and confess to you your mercies that it may praise you. Your entire creation never ceases to praise you and is never silent. Every spirit continually praises you with mouth turned towards you; animals and physical matter find a voice through those who contemplate them. So from weariness our soul rises towards you, first supporting itself on the created order and then passing on to you yourself who wonderfully made it. With you is restored strength and true courage.

(St Augustine)[1]

a meadow accepts itself as various, allows
some parts of itself to always be going away,
because whatever happens in that blown,

ragged field of grass and sway
is the meadow, and threading the frost
of its unlikely brilliance yesterday

we also were the meadow.

(Mark Doty, 'Becoming a Meadow')[2]

Knowing others

I have a little friend called Jacob. When I last saw him he was getting on for two years old, and feeling very proud of himself. As I arrived at the door he was beaming all over his face, excited, itching to show me something. And not just me, but anyone who would give him attention. Jacob had been swimming that morning with his Dad. Like any good father this father had persuaded eager little Jacob to go to the toilet in the changing rooms before entering the pool. Jacob had suddenly noticed that all the other boys there lined up at the urinal: they were doing 'stand up wees'. No way was Jacob sitting down to do his business; from henceforth he was doing 'stand up wees' like the big boys – and all the visitors to the house that day had to witness his new accomplishment, and spectate with appropriate rapture and approval as Jacob perched on his box by the downstairs loo grinning and shouting 'Look! Look! Stand up wees!', while one of his delighted parents tried to direct his inexperienced aim aright. He had yet to learn that his hands were needed!

What struck me in this performance was Jacob's sheer exuberance in his physical being – his total joy in the simple function of urinating, and his excitement as he discovers himself: his individuality, his capacity to do the various tasks of socialized human existence, his deepening participation in the community of human beings by going to the toilet. In doing his 'stand up wees' Jacob was becoming real to himself. Perhaps it is only as a child, and then much later in our lives, or when we are sick or infirm, that we recognize how important these bodily functions are, and what a joy it is to be able to fulfil them freely for oneself, as Jacob did (or almost!).

There was a time, when Jacob was younger, where if I picked him up, his tiny hands would be all over my face, his little fingers up my nose and in my eyes, bashing my spectacles, groping inside my mouth and scratching at my tongue and gums – an eager, vigorous process of probing, feeling, sensing where and what and who I was – a kind of mapping out reality through touch. This was an earlier process of 'stand up wees' as the child comes to know who he is in relation to others, knowing himself in and through knowing others. Now he is older, Jacob is learning that these others are persons, and that they have wants and needs and wills which are not subject to his own. This is a shocking lesson, and one which is ongoing for each of us: to find the boundaries of one's own personhood in learning the limits and demands of others. The novelist-philosopher Iris Murdoch suggests that knowing others and accepting their autonomous existence is what love is: 'Love is the perception of individuals. Love is the extremely difficult realization that something other than oneself is real. Love ... is the discovery of reality.'³ Jacob's probings, his physical feeling after others and himself, his first gropings and grapplings, soundings and spurtings which constitute his being of himself in relation to others, perhaps these are also his first feelings of love. He comes to know himself through knowing the reality of another, and as time goes on he learns that this reality implies that he is not the central focus of all existence, but a precious part of its complex and wonderful whole.

Rather strangely, when I was part of the audience crowded into the doorway of the lavatory that day, I thought of an enclosed and silent community of nuns which I had once visited. I had in my mind the picture of a sister walking noiselessly and deliberately down a long corridor in the convent, a sight which had puzzled me greatly at the time. I remember asking myself questions about their life together: Why do they live in silence? Why do they move and do every action and say every word so carefully? Why have they chosen to live their lives so bound up with others, governed by rules and regulations for almost every aspect of human activity?

Watching Jacob, I began to see what this strict form of religious life might be about. It struck me that these sisters unpick all that they have learned about being human – all the social practices of being human are deconstructed and reconstructed within community so that the purposes of God may be known in them and played out through them. Talking, eating, sleeping, forming relationships, having sexual attractions and repulsions, these are no longer conceived of as mere functions or habits, a matter of compulsion or taboo; they become, ideally at least, the stuff of love in which human beings may know and serve others and The Other, who is God. The individual acknowledges that she does not live by herself for herself, but that she lives with and through her sisters, sustained by God. In acknowledging this, she choses to live *for* them and for God, and she knows herself as a person intimately connected with others and with God.

One understanding of this form of religious life is as a way of discipleship which pays radical attention to 'the other'. Perhaps by concentrating on the patterns of human existence, and in acknowledging their interdependence, those sisters are able to experience the joy of human being in something like the way that Jacob can, and also something of the pain of broken and divided humanity. Theirs is a radical rediscovery of embodied self in relation to God and one another. They live a life which fosters profound attentiveness within the self to God and to the life of creation.

Religious communities symbolize the contemplative life, a quality which may thrive beyond the formal structures of religion, even as religion may sometimes be its suppressor. Sally McFague has described contemplation as a way of knowing, what she calls *attention epistemology*: knowledge from attending to someone or something other than oneself, respecting that 'other' as it is in itself, without calculating its utilitarian value. This way of knowing is a kind of meditative practice, an example of which McFague finds in a description given by Iris Murdoch as she attends to 'the sheer, alien pointless independent existence of animals, birds, stones, and trees':

> I am looking out of my window in an anxious and resentful state of mind, brooding perhaps on some damage done to my prestige. Then suddenly I observe a hovering kestrel. In a moment everything is altered. The brooding self with its hurt vanity has disappeared. There is nothing but kestrel. And when I return to thinking of the other matter it seems less important.[4]

For McFague, this way of seeing the world is a way of knowing oneself as a part of it, rather than as its centre. It is a process of recognizing the real, the activity of loving, of appreciating the variety and radical particularity of the teeming life of the planet. This seems to me to be a mode of prayer, a probing of the world which gives birth to a thankful and joyful recognition of its being beyond ourselves, and – for those who have eyes to see and ears to hear – a recognition of The Other who is its creator and sustainer. This is a kind of meditative reaching out, a finding of perspective, of knowing one's humanity within the life of the universe through 'paying attention, listening to, learning about the specialness, the difference, the detail of the "wonderful life" of which we are a part'.[5]

The contemplative eye will see the *difference* between all living things, and at the same time their *connectedness*. It will see what is distinctive or unique, and yet how one form of life relates to another. Contemplation discovers independence and interdependence, fostering knowledge of and respect for life in its variety and relationality. Those who look with this contemplative eye will see the differences between human persons and locate this multifarious humanity within the network of manifold life-forms, not dominating or exploiting, but seeking to co-exist as 'stewards of life's continuity on earth',[6] and fulfilling the human vocation to 'solidarity with all other creatures of the earth, especially the vulnerable and needy ones'.[7]

For Christians, argues McFague, this *ecological* model of the radical particularity and interrelatedness of all being must replace the organic model of unity which envisages 'the whole' as a single body – particularly the community of the church modelled as the Body of Christ. This body has too often been defined as the ideal male body, a symbol of heterosexual male experience which is universalized as the norm. This model of the single (male) body then operates to include or exclude, approve or disapprove, imposing a masculinized unity which is based – like masculine identity – on a fear and loathing of that which it is not: not woman, not gay, not black. Organic unity which is envisaged as a single body can suggest a limitation of diversity. That which disturbs the unity of this body must be excluded or conformed.

McFague offers a new analogy for organic unity: the universe imagined as God's body – that is, the unity of the multiplicity of different bodies in the universe as they are sustained by the loving, creative power of the transcendent God. This is the unity of all interrelated, multiplying life which receives life from the life of God. This model has the appeal of being ecological, a model which draws those who are inspired by it away from the anthropocentric and androcentric tendencies of the unity implied by the Body of Christ. Yet the contemplative outlook suggests that the unity implied by the church as Body of Christ need not be interpreted as an exclusive unity. For those who know the radical particularity of being – including their own particularity in relation to others – will have respect for the diversity of being; they will want to cherish difference rather than obliterate or dominate other forms of life.

As we have seen, the masculine body theology of James B. Nelson encourages men to befriend their bodies and to find within them the diversity of manhood – to recognize the different, complimentary qualities which are represented in the erect and the flaccid penis: a contemplation of embodied masculinity. This contemplation re-unites the spiritual and the sexual/physical – it makes 'the intimate connection' – the many ways of being and desiring grounded in the male body which together combine in 'being a man'. Men who contemplate their bodies are no longer alienated from them or afraid of the differences which constitute their masculinity; their bodies cease to be tools, to be idealized or objectified, and become integrated into the totality of a man's being, with an attendant respect for other embodied being.

Nelson initiates this body theology in his contemplation of the body of Jesus, known not as an asexual being, but as a man with penis and testicles, a particular *gendered* being. It seems to me that men who know the particularity of their own bodies are less likely to universalize male experience, and from this knowledge, are more free to allow the metaphor of the Body of Christ to do its work in relation to the particular body of Jesus of Nazareth, born of Mary. Knowing themselves as they are, accepting their diversity as men, then men are less in need of universalizing their experience in such a way that it denies the reality of others. They can recognize that the resurrected Christ is not a projection of themselves, a sovereign male, but one who is the cosmic Christ – 'the Christ freed from the body of Jesus of Nazareth, to be present in and to all bodies'.[8] The reconciliation which began in the incarnation of God in the particular, male body of Jesus, the man who died and rose from the dead, is fulfilled in the ascended and glorified Body of Christ, in which all bodies are gathered up and transformed. The Body of Christ is a redemptive body in which all life, in all its teeming difference, is honoured, welcomed, loved, and fulfilled. This Body is much greater than the male body of Jesus, and yet it is the fruit of that particular life which embodied the human and the divine in perfect co-relation and harmony.

> He himself is before all things, and in him all things hold together. He is the head of the body, the church; he is the beginning, the first born from the dead, so that he might come to have first place in everything. For in him the fullness of God was pleased to dwell, and through him God was pleased to reconcile to himself all things, whether on earth or in heaven, by making peace through the blood of his cross (Colossians 1.17–20).

Human being as relationship

This contemplative way of knowing oneself within a world of difference may sound like a practice which is foreign among men, to be encouraged as a programme of ethical improvement. Yet the doctrine of human beings made in the image of God suggests that persons are such by virtue of their interrelatedness and interdependence. For the God whom we mirror is Trinity, community, three persons who are a unity of mutual relationship. This doctrine enshrines what Jacob's physical and social explorations in toileting embody: that human beings are relational, knowing themselves physically, sexually, psychologically and spiritually, in and through another. This is what defines human personhood:

> The analogy between God and human existence in the image is … not one of individual sustance but of relation. Just as the Persons of the Trinity receive and maintain their identities through relation, and relations of a certain quality,

then so would human persons only receive and maintain their identities through relations with others and would stand fully in God's image whenever these identities and relations achieved a certain quality.[9]

McFadyen interprets the project of redemption as the restoration of the *quality* of human relationships to that of the life of the Trinity, for whom difference between persons generates love rather than fear. For him the doctrines of the fall and original sin describe the distortion of human being through the breakdown of right relationships with God and one another.[10] In the incarnation of God in Jesus Christ, the fullness of God reaches out, communicates, with those whose communication is distorted. The calling of the church is to be a foretaste of these redeemed relations which are patterned by Jesus Christ, a community whose life is characterized by a radical openess to God and to one another. What McFadyen envisages is a dynamic process of continuing dialogue in which 'the partners are simultaneously independent ... and inseparably bound together in a search for mutuality of under-standing'.[11]

This is an ecclesial task of apprehension and response, of learning one's own needs and desires and how to relate them justly to the needs and desires of others – including the needs of life other than humanity, the interconnected life of the planet. This is a calling to become a contemplative church, a church which fosters unity through acknowledging, embracing, restoring, and strengthening right relationship among diverse life. Yet it has been mainly women who have begun to imagine the shape of such a church. Robert Bly wrote *Iron John* because he finds that so many men are lacking insight and foresight, whilst women are abounding in a creative energy which men demonstrably lack. So are men consigned to self-absorption and the struggle to fight off resentment, rather than being involved in renewal and transformation?

There are men who are articulating a vision of a future church which is a community of dialogue, men such as Hans Küng, Desmond Tutu, and Donald Reeves. Their writings and practical efforts show that these are men who are in creative dialogue with groups of women, gay people, ecologists, in seeking to build partnerships which sustain diverse life.[12] If men are in need of new heroes to inspire them for the current age, as some of the literature on masculinity suggests, then the heroic should be re-imagined as these men are displaying their masculinities: as contemplative and amicable, seeking mutual respect and understanding. A world of difference needs men and women who can help us live together in peace and justice.

There remains the question whether men are able to be participators rather than controllers. I think there are signs that a new man is emerging – not the superficial new man who is new enough to sell cars and cosmetics, but men, both gay and straight, black and white, believers and non-believers, who are doing the hard and honest work of reconsidering themselves in the company of women, and who are doing so mindful of the needs of the planet. These are men who are genuinely participating with women in the running of households and families, churches, charities and organizations of all kinds.

Signs of hope: being together

Recently I was participating in a service in church which I found particularly moving. Why it should seem so puzzled me. Though I was a visitor to the church and congregation, nothing I experienced there was strange to me. It was a smallish group of people gathered in a cherished, familiar sort of neo-Gothic building. The liturgy was thoughtful, reverent, authentic – in this sense very special, but not unknown to me in its form, or emotive in a deliberate way.

The vicar of this church was a woman, and the priest presiding that day was also a woman. The organist was a woman, and all the officers of the church whom I had met beforehand were women too. A man conducted the choir, and men read the scriptures and led the intercessions. I was the preacher. The congregation was a mixture of people from the local community, women and men, young and old and most of what comes in between. A good mix. I had come across similar congregations before, and yet this place seemed so full of energy and promise – to me, quite extraordinarily so.

Indeed, this parish is experiencing a renewal after many years of decline. The vicar has worked with others – mostly women – to revitalize the church. Though they are still a tiny proportion of the population of their town, managing with meagre finances, they have restructured their building, demolishing some parts of it and renovating others; they have welcomed children back to the congregation, encouraged parents and single people – anyone who wishes to come along is welcomed and valued, it seems. They are a happy, realistic congregation who are making an outreach to people in their local community, particularly to groups who are vulnerable or over-looked. Yet whilst I appreciated all of this activity, I think it was their way of being together that affected me. It was the quality of their relations – what seemed to be a spirit of partnership, mutual respect and tolerance.

I am sure that much of this is due to the skill and devotion of the vicar and the key members who work with her. But what impressed me was their lack of rivalry. It was not as if they operated with a sense that women were taking control where men had failed, but that women had initiated a partnership in the church which was inclusive rather than exclusive. This practice was symbolized in the eucharist as the priest (a woman) broke the bread for the women, children and men who stood around her in a body of different bodies – a life of lives which gathers to receive new life. There was a multiplicity of persons, each distinct, drawn together into one life, one body, whilst remaining themselves and becoming more fully themselves as they acknowledge their belonging one with another in the shared brokeness of the body-bread. I dare say that in that group, just as in any group, there are wrangles over power, misunderstandings, conscious or unconscious disunities. Though it seemed to me an excellent church, it cannot be perfect; and even so, because it is so, as that church offers and breaks and shares the bread in that sacramental moment of interrelationship, I sensed that I was sharing in the creation of a new church and a new world. The eucharist was an anticipation of restored relationships, and I had sensed something of what Gutierrez calls 'confidence that the communion of life that does not yet exist among us can become a reality'. Nor is this gathering of different people into one body of openess and response an evasion of our divisions – or at least, it need not be so, for the eucharist 'represents an acknowledgment that the gift of life by the risen Christ concerns every moment and every area of human existence'.[13]

If the men's movement is to have any influence within the churches, whether that be in the form of men's groups and an awareness of 'men's issues', or of a focus on 'masculine spirituality', or of a particular outreach to men, then its business must be about encouraging men to participate with women in these anticipations of restored relationships. Men must be encouraged to combine with women in mutual respect and work creatively with them, in dialogue. The starting point of this dialogue for men may not be a louder assertion of men's needs but, rather, a de-centring of themselves which begins in a recognition of women's needs and gifts, and an acknowledgment of the ways in which men harm others, including children and gay people. But this repentance needs to be authentic, initiated in listening – which must include attending carefully to the pain within boys and men who feel themselves to have been harmed.

Men must speak for themselves about themselves. Part of the restoring of relationships is to foster places where men can confront their feelings and behaviour and break the silence of their anger, fear or grief. Situations in which men can dredge up from within themselves so much of what they suppress, or to which they give inappropriate expression in violence, abuse, and addiction, or in which they can challenge those accepted patterns of maleness which are degrading. Situations such as these are part of the healing of relations. But they will not be places of healing if they generate a culture of women being blamed so that men may safely evade their responsibilities.

Nor is this healing all confessional in form. Men and women are working creatively together in the kind of 'alliance politics' which Bob Connell envisaged. One example I know well is a charity working with and for homeless people in which the Executive Director, Chair of Council, and a majority of the Trustees are women. Some men in the organization have found women's leadership difficult, not least their open and non-confrontational style of negotiation and management. Yet in practice, this is an organization where men and women of goodwill come together to respond to human need as it presents itself in homelessness. Certainly this need is gendered: homeless women have requirements which differ from those of homeless men, and the causes of their homelessness often differ; yet these needs can be recognized and sensitively met so that difference does not give rise to injustice. In the same way, women workers and managers may have requirements and styles which differ from those of men, but where the established norm is sensitivity, flexibility and mutual respect – a situation of dialogue – then the organization functions efficiently and humanely. Difference enhances rather than diffuses the energy and effectiveness of the body when an organization puts contemplation into practice.

In his poem 'Becoming a Meadow', Mark Doty pictures himself in a bookshop in a seaside town in a snow storm, remembering a walk he took with his lover on the shore, at a place called 'Head of the Meadow'. Like many of Doty's poems, this poem is infused with the presence of HIV disease. Death is very much part of living. As the shop door-bell jangles, it rings in the poet's head as the phrase 'becoming a meadow', and the bookshop becomes for him a waving and bobbing as its plethora of words, its languages and meanings, blow like grasses in the wind, being made and remade – like the meadow – by those who enter and read and write their own stories with its stories. And then the meadow of grass becomes a meadow of water:

one filling and emptying wave, spilling and pulling back,
and everything waves are: dissolving, faster,
only to swell again.

The poet speaks a vision of interconnected meanings, of a
body of worlds – social, intellectual, erotic, physical, chemical
– which form one world in all its shifting, settling, breaking,
mending continuity and change. This is a contemplative
poem, one which sees the multiplicity of things as they are in
themselves and as they relate to others – without which they
would have no meaning or existence and yet, in the company
of which, they thrive and so vibrantly *are*. This vision is a 'sort
of answer': provisional, realist, fantastic, nourishing, dimin-
ishing and demanding – not imposing order, but somehow
finding it within the continual transpositions of being:

And if one wave breaking says
You're dying, then the rhythm and shift of the whole
says nothing about endings, and half the shawling head

of each wave's spume pours into the trough
of the one before,
and half blows away in spray, backward, toward the open sea.

These are the words of a man who contemplates a world of
difference; who finding his place within it, knows himself to
belong with others in a constant relationship of encounter and
transition, and in so knowing is thereby continually becoming
himself.

8

On Silence

One of the good things about being a man is that men can be silent.

Privatized, subjectivized ineffable mysticism ... keeps God (and women) safely out of politics and the public realm; it allows mysticism to flourish as a secret inner life, while those who nurture such an inner life can generally be counted on to prop up rather than to challenge the status quo of their work places, their gender roles, and the political systems by which they are governed, since their anxieties and angers will be allayed in the privacy of their own hearts' search for peace and tranquility.

(Grace Jantzen)[1]

If you dare to penetrate your own silence ... then you will truly recover the light and the capacity to understand what is beyond words ... that you and He are in all truth One Spirit.

(Thomas Merton)[2]

Looking into the face of Christ

On the cover of this book is the face of Christ painted by Georges Rouault: 'Christ aux Outrages' – Christ mocked. It is the face of one who is silent: the face of man, the face of God. This is the face of Christ who has been betrayed and handed over to the religious and secular authorities, the face of a man who stands battered by a cacophany of accusation, interrogation, verbal and physical assault. The passion narratives, as they describe the scenes of Christ's questioning by Pilate and Herod, his brutal humiliation by the soldiers and his denunciation by the crowds and the religious leaders, paint the picture of a man who is surrounded by words, a man who suffers the lash and probe of many searing voices, whose response is largely one of silence. Here is the face of Christ who is mocked in a storm of language, but he does no speaking.

> Now the men who were holding Jesus mocked him and beat him; they also blindfolded him and asked him, 'Prophesy! Who is it that struck you?' And they spoke many other words against him, reviling him (Luke 22.63–65).[3]

We see the face of a man who is silent as he undergoes the most appalling humiliation. Is this the face of despair that we see? Is this the look of a man abandoned, bewildered, despised and self-despising, the blank face masking pain and terror? Is this silence the speechlessness of a man who looks into the depths of human evil and cruelty, the silence of a man confronted by the prospect of his death at the hands of those who are completely merciless, utterly blind to God's purposes of love and peace? Have their mockeries undone within him all he ever had to say? Perhaps their screams, their slaps and punches, perhaps they have broken down the language of love which was easy to speak on the hill-top and in the fields? Has Christ come within himself to a place where words run out? Has he come to a place of utter despair, to godlessness, to the wilderness where there are no brothers or sisters, no hope, no love? Why is Christ silent? How is this silence to be interpreted? What does his silence say?

This same silence of Christ mocked, is this also the sign of his complete obedience to God's will? Is it the silence of one who is to take all hatred and evil upon himself willingly, though he is guiltless? Is this the silence of the sacrificial victim, a silence which is to be heard as assent (Isaiah 53.7ff.; I Peter 2.18ff.)? Are we to imitate this silence as the model for our own behaviour? Is this the meaning of the silence?

In this silence of the Christ who is mocked, do we meet the 'gaze of love', the searching, knowing look of God who is encountered in the silence, who 'sees us in our absolute truth, and seeing us … loves us and brings us to blissful fulfilment'?[4] Is this place of despair also the discovery of hope? What is the meaning of his silence? What are we to make of it? How are we to respond?

The dangerous rubric: 'Silence may be kept … '

Silence is not neutral. Silence is not uniform. Silences differ. Silences may be chosen, or they may be endured. Silences may be imposed, or they may be sought. Silences are a matter for interpretation, they are communication – they are given different meanings and they assume different significances. For some, silence is an absence of words; for others, a defiance of talk. For one man, a resting, a healing, a basking, an emptying, a being filled, a place of calm, a nothingness. For another, silence is a censoring, a struggle, a constipation, a barreness, a place of pain, an agony unable to break free in tears or fury. Silence may be full or empty; it may be passive or active; it may be intended for good or for harm, it may be fallen into like a trap, or like the Everlasting Arms. Silence may be the attack or the defence, a refuge or an assault. It may be shelter, it may be evasion. Silence may be for seeing, for insight and understanding, a place of gift; it may be a place of prayer, of community, of communion, of being with others in their joy or their pain, a place of strengthening. Or silence may be a dreadful turning away, a closing of the mind and the heart, a practice of rejection, a denial; it may be the absence of God and alienation from others, a place of isolation, of loss, of disintegration. It may be some or all of these at different times, at one and the same time.

Silence is never saying nothing. Silence is always more than the absence of language; it has a place within language, and each silence resonates with other silences, endorsing or rejecting them, drawing alongside or running away. There is no 'holy silence' which is separated off from other silences, as if the silence of worship or contemplative prayer were holy ground on which no living thing would dare to tread. In the silence we may encounter Love. In the silence we may find the realities of our injustices, pain and despair, and we may not be sure – in the silence – whether we are basking in 'the gaze of love', or being scrutinized by the condemning stare. In the silence our guilt and self hatred rise up and make their own interpretations. Does love burn, or are we in hell?

In his 'Letter on the Contemplative Life' Thomas Merton describes his life of solitude and silence as a search in the despair and pain which men and women experience deep within themselves, but which they seldom 'visit'.

I have been summoned to explore a desert area of man's heart in which explanations no longer suffice, and in which one learns that only experience counts. An arid, rocky, dark land of the soul, sometimes illuminated by strange fires which men fear and peopled by spectres which men studiously avoid except in their nightmares. And in this area I have learned that one cannot truly know hope unless he has found out how like despair hope is.[5]

Being a contemplative, Merton is not glib about silence. His journey into silence has not been an escape from the suffering of the world, a post-Holocaust, post-Hiroshima world in which certainties have fallen away. In the silence he comes face to face with the doubts and desperation of his fellow men and women. Yet knowing how dangerous this search is, he encourages those who are seeking meaning and purpose in a world which is traumatized by the destructiveness of human evil and the corruption of religion to attend to the silence within themselves. Though he knows how much guilt and self-hatred and doubt and violence are to be encountered on the journey within, even so he asks, 'Do we dare to penetrate our silences?' Do we dare, in the silence, to come face to face with human pain and human sorrow, and to discover the hope which lies among them, close by them? For the hurting is the pain of a God who longs to be in union with human beings – God present within each human being, loving him, and being made known in the loving of human relationships:

It is the love of my lover, my brother or my child that sees God in me, makes God credible to myself in me. And it is my love for my lover, my child, my brother, that enables me to show God to him or her in himself or herself. Love is the epiphany of God in our poverty. The contemplative life is then the search for peace not in an abstract exclusion of all outside reality, not in a barren negative closing of the senses upon the world, but in the openness of love.[6]

The journey inwards takes Merton outwards towards the fabric of relationship and human interaction. In contemplation, the commerce of human loving and the depths of inner silence meet.

Penetrating silence: sifting through the silences of men

Among men, the practice of silence is nuanced. Men keep silent about silence. Of the many silences that men keep, here are three: the silence of suicide; the silence of unemployment; the silence of poverty.

The silence of suicide

When those who heard were told, the place was immediately familiar to them. The reservoir had always been popular for days out. They had known it since they were kids. They had even been there together last summer, Dave and the lads. Dave had brought his own child there too, with Sue, on one of the first weekends after she and the baby had come home. But mostly it was with the lads that he had been there – somewhere to go and have a laugh, a place to drive to, to fish if you could afford the licence or didn't mind the risk of getting caught by the gamie. Somewhere to go and sit on the wall at the top of the dam, have a fag, break open a couple of cans, look back across the water to the hills, or over and down the long length of stone to the foot of the wet rock and the water channel rushing away. From there you could drop stones, listen to the silence of them falling, hear them smack at the bottom with a loud crack.

So there was no strangeness about the place – they could picture it immediately: the long twist of dark water between the hills, the pine woods coming right down to the road which wound all the way around the lake for miles. The silence. Especially the silence at night, with no traffic, no town near by, no people – just the sound of the water gushing at the foot of the dam and the faint mechanical noise of the pumps some- where way underground, not to be seen. At night the only lights were in the pump house down the valley, and a few distant glimmers from the houses on the hillside. Otherwise, darkness by the dam, and the quiet.

He wasn't a loud man, Dave. There was music in the car, of course, and in his room, and the radio while he was working. Just him up the scaffolding and Radio One to keep him com- pany. A quiet lad by nature, but not shy. Nothing odd about him. In the pub he was a laugh, got cheekier with beer, had a hell of a way with women, could shout like hell on the football field. But he kept his own counsel. Was a dark horse. Deep. Not even Sue would know sometimes what was going on in that head. There was a bit of talk about the business a time ago – money problems, late payers, things a bit sluggish – but he was working all the hours God sends – sometimes seventy, eighty, a hundred hours a week when he could. He was over- doing it really, pushing himself too hard. But he had to take the work while it was there. We couldn't see the pressure, what was going on inside. He was out for his pint pretty much as usual, and a session now and then. Nothing strange. Some say now he was a bit too quiet , but then they would, now it's happened, now it's too late. He said nothing to nobody. Kept it all to himself.

So it was a shock, hearing – how he'd gone out as usual, and hadn't come home, how Sue was ringing round all the mates, worried sick, and how one of the reservoir men had come across him in the morning, at the bottom, on the rock, and how the coppers had come and Dan had had to go to the mortuary because Sue was in such a state. We all wondered what he must have looked like, knowing how far down it was from the wall to the rock at the bottom. But none of us said anything, and Dan was saying nothing in the pub: shock, it was, after the identification. Later we heard that he'd folded his clothes on the top and put his watch on the wall there with them, carefully, like normal, and the car keys too – as if he was going for a swim after that very long dive, all tidy. Calm. And we talked about that for weeks and weeks, wondering what it was that got to him, what was in his head to make him give up Sue and the kids and the house and the business. And his mates. Whether it was a mistake. He said nothing to anyone. Not to any of us, not even to Sue, nor his Mum and Dad, nor Dan. Nothing. We felt like there must have been something he said, some signal to let us know how it was. Something we'd missed. But none of us could remember him saying a word. He let nothing out. That was the biggest shock really, just hearing that he'd done it. On his own, in the night, up there, in the quiet. It was very brave of him. It takes a lot of guts to do a thing like that.

But I can't help wondering if he shouted as he fell.

The silence of unemployment

From the houses in this cul-de-sac you could hear the noise of the works day and night every week of the year except Christmas and Summer. Nobody noticed it 'till it stopped. Then there was quiet – beautiful for a while, like holiday with the money from the pay-off too – then all the crashing of the demolition as they took down the works and rolled out the ground, put up new fences. Then the quiet again. Then the reality of it set in.

Every day I'd worked since I was fourteen. First in the pits down in South Wales like my father and brothers and uncles. Then we came up here for the steel. Hard work. Hellish sometimes – the heat and the muck – but better than the pits. Good money too. Thousands of men at this site. The whole estate was working there at the mills, or in one of the plants connected with it. Straight from school at sixteen to the works. Straight from the works to the pubs on a Friday. We would take twelve thousand quid in a couple of hours on a Friday at the Working Men's Club. They would come pouring out of the gates and in through the doors, gagging for it. Thirsty work. Plenty of money about then. Plenty of life in the place. People spending down the town, going on trips, family nights in the Club, coaches to Blackpool, bowls, snooker, darts, pigeons, great stonking rows in Branch Meetings, a laugh with your mates, something to get up for every day, something to recover from when you got home, money to buy the kids whatever they wanted. Nobody went without. Everyone knew where they were in life. There was somewhere you knew the kids could go when they needed a job – down the works, on the floor or in the offices. At times it was shit. It wouldn't be right for everybody, but if you were the ordinary type of bloke, that place would have seen you alright. There's nothing now. The town's dead.

I don't go on about it, but I get a bit low sometimes. Sixty-one I am now; eleven years since the works closed. It's been rough at times, when it began to dawn on me that there was nothing else coming along. There was a load of talk about re-training, but nothing came of it. Nothing is going to come neither. I worry about the kids. And now the kids are having kids without never having worked. It's crazy, a waste. We're storing up trouble for ourselves.

Don't get me wrong: I've made the best of it; I'm busy with the allotment and at the Club, helping to keep things going there. But it's quiet, no money, the kids aren't interested in belonging. There's nothing for 'em. I couldn't lie in bed 'till two like some of them do, watching videos all day, some of them younger ones on drugs, robbing cars to pay for them, buggering the place up. But what do they have? What have they got to look forward to? What's the future hold for them? I can get up in the morning. For me it's routine. Years of work. Can't stand festering in bed. I get up and fetch the paper and help Her with the house-work; we'll walk up town for the smallest thing, hunt around the shops for the bargains. We get a buzz out of watching the pennies. We walk miles in a week. I haven't got fat like some of them. I try not to get under her feet. I think she likes having me about the place now, but it was hell for a while, bickering, seeing too much of one another, missing the company of men at the works, not being able to get out of the house – not in the winter, not just to walk the streets.

It's taken me a long time to accept that not everything depends on me, and that what I was taught to do as a young man – to work hard for as long as I had to, and to do the best for my family that way – isn't much use now. And in most of these houses on this estate there will be men watching telly all day who've had to accept the same, and some of them have gone down with it. It's a tough lesson to learn. It rots the guts to think that you're not really needed. There's a lot of suffering behind those front doors. But now I've learned to get out of the house whatever the weather, rain or shine. Even in snow. Now I know that the afternoons will drive me mad if I sit there in the quiet reading the paper over and over, staring through the window across to the empty space beyond the fence, remembering what used to be, feeling angry or useless or something. That's when the silence would really get to me.

The silence of poverty

My name is Babu Paranandi. Like my father, I am a casual labourer. I must have been eight years old when my father decided to uproot himself from Bombay and go to the Gulf. He did it to earn enough money to secure the future of his four children. Six months later his body arrived back – without life and without money – and we had become destitutes overnight.

Poverty was nothing new to us. It was poverty that prompted my father, an illiterate farmer, to leave his land and his family in Andhra Pradesh and board a train for Bombay. My mother accompanied him with my one-year-old sister. For the next seven or eight years they worked on construction sites earning a joint wage of fifty or sixty rupees a day. On this they had to keep their daughter and three sons. I am the eldest boy.

It was after the birth of the fourth child that my father

decided to move to Dubai. Though no one knows the truth behind his death, I do remember that my mother's immediate concern was to find ways of feeding four hungry mouths. The only solace was the roof over our heads. I admire my mother. Our relatives started to shun us. Instead of returning to our native village and working in the fields, she decided to stay and face an uncertain future.

When I was eight years old – the age when other children are into studies and sports – I had to earn money to support the family, as I was the eldest son. And that is how it has been ever since.

My first job was as a florist's delivery boy. Part of the day I attended lessons, the rest of the time I was making garlands and delivering them to various houses. I earned twenty rupees a month. I could not afford to carry on studying. I became a labourer at a construction site. While my mother was paid twenty-five rupees a day for carting bricks, I shifted heavy slabs for fifty rupees a day. From our earnings we paid for my brothers' schooling, and for food. We managed to save a little. When building work halts in the monsoons we would have no money for food. Do you want to know what poverty is? It is eating borrowed rice mixed with salt and red pepper chutney.

The best days of my life were spent working in a social club where I was jack-of-all-trades. For three years I worked day and night, washing utensils, sweeping floors and running errands for the men who would play cards there. The chores brought me twenty-five rupees a day, but I would earn sixty rupees running errands for the gamblers. Those were the good days because I forced my mother to stop working and I managed to become the sole breadwinner for the family.

But the good times don't last for ever. The club closed down and we were back to square one. For a year I had no job. My brother Stya had to leave school and find a job. He earned a thousand rupees a month for twelve hours work, seven days a week. My mother also had to start working again. Then fate struck another blow. Six months into her pregnancy my sister had a miscarriage and had to be hospitalized. We had to beg and borrow money to pay for her treatment. And hardly had we brought her home than her husband fell under a train and was killed. Life was hell.

Creditors were knocking at the door. I desperately hunted for a job. I became a *mathadi*. My job is to load and unload cement bags. I get paid one hundred and fifty-five rupees a day. It is back-breaking work, but I stick to it as I have my family to feed. But as I am not a permanent employee, I get work only three or four days a week. If I became a member of the union I could get a permanent badge. But for that I need thirty thousand rupees. From where do I get so much money? I am nineteen and sometimes I feel desperate. My mother is getting old. I have a sister to re-marry, and I want my brothers to complete their studies and get decent jobs. Where can I earn enough money for all of this? The only option is to return to our village, Nalagada, and cultivate the land. But the problem is we don't know how to work the land any more.[7]

When there is so much hidden in silence, it may be that men should consider their silences: search them out, submit them for examination, learn the variety of them, make friends even with those we would rather not know. For not every silence among men is good, as any man who has been bullied or ignored or threatened will know. Men will know the occasions when they have imposed silence as an end to challenges of their power, or when they have used silence as an emotional weapon, or when they have struggled to maintain a silence rather than risk an expression of feelings which leaves them vulnerable.

If we penetrate the silence, then we shall find that there is a silence which accompanies the lustful gaze – a leering, pos-sessing silence. There is a silence which accompanies disdain, disapproval, denigration, dismissal – the silence of racism, misogyny, homophobia, snobbery. There is the silence which preceeds violence. There is a silence which is the blank silence of a man dead to himself and to others. There is a silence among men which forbids expression – silence which stiffles the asking of a question, which outlaws challenge, difference, dissent. This is the silence of terror, a silence which smothers any talk of change, any exploration of the truth. This is the silence which denies vision and will not answer complaint. This is the silence of deliberately not hearing others, a silence which enforces the silence of others. This is the silence which the powerful man enjoys.

There is the silence of a man who cannot tell his pain, his grief, his fear, his anger, his loathing, his joy, his desire, his longing, his love. This silence is about not knowing what there is to say and not knowing how to say it – the silence of a man who has no connection with his feelings, who cannot interpret the language of his body. This is the silence of a man who may listen to others but cannot listen to himself.

There is the silence of attack and punishment among men, the silence which retaliates by saying nothing, in refusing to negotiate or to discuss or to say what another longs to hear – the silence of withholding forgiveness, love, recognition, praise, apology, consolation. There are men who can use silence like fists.

There is the silence of collusion, a silence which joins with unjust silence in saying nothing when wrong is done, a silence which participates in not challenging violence, prejudice, ignorance, exploitation. This silence lets others remain unfairly accused or misunderstood; it permits evil. This is a silence which will not admit fault, nor accept responsibility, a silence which covers exploitation and sanctions abuse. This is the silence of privilege, self-satisfaction, denial: the profitable silence, the silence of lies. This silence is louder than the cries of the poor.

And those whose cries are not heard have their own silence, the silence of many millions of men and women and children who are so exhausted by the relentlessness of their work, so numbed by their hunger or their cold or defeated by the fruitlessness of their search for labour, for security, for a safe place for their refugee families, that talking is too much of a luxury, a function which is simply beyond them as they struggle with the brutality and weight of the injustice they suffer. This is the silence of the poor.

And there is the silence of the outsider, of the persecuted, the victim – a silence of fear, of shame, of swallowing words and restraining argument because of the threat of violence or ridicule. This is the silence which protects a life, a job, an identity, a home; a silence surrounding the dignity and security of self or another person from the brutality of denunciation, persecution, physical and sexual assault. This is the silence of necessity, adversity – a sheltering silence, a silence which is bitter and burns inside. This is the silence of the bullied and abused.

The bridge of silence

Men's silence can be harmful, destructive, unkind. It may be a barrier, a weapon, a threat, an evasion, a protection: the product of fear or dysfunction, the signal of division within a man, and within relationships and communities. In silence a man can be hiding from the realities of his power, of the injustice which power creates and sustains. But there is also a silence which listens and absorbs what another has to say and who another person is. A silence which accommodates, which makes space for welcome. A silence which is about resting in the body without having to be always talking, telling, responding; an accepting silence. There is sometimes a mutuality among men which finds expression in silence. Silence as a shared experience, as a time of appreciation and pleasure in others, of being with others. Sometimes a man is silent not because he is terrified of others, but because that is a way of being with them. His silence is a bridge rather than a barrier. As Merton found, silence may be a way toward others and toward the reality of self and God rather than a retreat from relationship and community.

Perhaps because silence is the mask and the cover for so much which is vulnerable, men are reluctant to explore their silences. But this silence about silence is fostering misunderstanding and inappropriate shame among men. There are silences which are creative rather than stifling, spaces where compassion and friendship may flourish. Sometimes this realization emerges among men when the nature of men's silence is questioned by women in a situation which is 'safe' for the men. For example, during a training day for clergy exploring issues concerning men and masculinity I repeated an exercise which I had experienced with the theologian James B. Nelson. The exercise involves groups of men and women listening to one another. Each group would discuss its own sex: what they enjoyed about being male or female. First the women sat in a group together and talked about what they valued in being women, whilst the men listened. Then the men talked together about what they valued in being men whilst the women listened. Then the two groups exchanged impressions of the conversations they had heard.

What the men had to say about the women's group was fairly predictable: it seemed to the men that the women had formed an intimacy very readily; they were open to one another, listened well, talked freely, responded spontaneously and sensitively. The women were at home in expressing their sense of themselves as women – they could talk bodies, feelings, sex; they could articulate need, desire, dissatisfaction, pleasure; they could tolerate the differences between them without threat, they seemed comfortable and strong in the variety of ways in which they were women. They could talk about themselves without reference to men. And the women concurred with these observations and impressions.

What the women had to say about the men was also rather predictable: the men seemed to be uncomfortable with one another. There was a lot of laughter and joking in the group but very little genuine conversation – a sense of the men evading what was difficult for them, hedging around the tricky issues of identity and sexuality. Lots of guffawing about penises – a mixture of bravado and insecurity. The men were faltering in their expressions, the conversation seemed superficial; perhaps the task of self-revelation left them exposed and vulnerable, lost for words? There were a great many silences. Were the men in agony, or anxious, or repressed?

But the men felt very differently about their group. They felt that the usual discomfort that men might have in 'going personal' with other men had subsided very quickly, and that there was a sense of openness and acceptance in the group, and that the laughter was about the absurdities of the conventions which so often hedged men in – a laughter which they had never experienced with other men before, and an openness about the body and sexuality which they had never had with a variety of other men before. And the silences were expressed as times of acceptance and safety and mutual appreciation rather than the product of terror. Those particular silences were the signal of men being open and receptive and feeling comfortable with one another.

Of course the men may have said what they said as a way of being right, of retaining control and defending themselves from what they interpreted as negative criticism. It may have been an occasion of men mystifying their relationships with one another to obscure from women the alienation and powerlessness they felt in that situation. But such defensive responses would not have been in the spirit of a day in which those same men had been very open with the women about the difficulties they experienced in being men. The men had talked with one another about the struggles which they had as men to retain or to escape the stereotypical roles of conventional masculinity.

Rather, the men felt that the women had helped them begin to understand something which they had not appreciated before, what one man called *the coded nature of men's communication* – codes which are not easily understood, which are learnt and have to be interpreted, and which may serve in many varying situations to exclude women and some men, whilst including others. For these codes are about power. But the codes also form a careful language allowing for disclosure and mutuality and intimacy among men in tentative, guarded ways. For the men in that particular group, the silences were about men beginning to feel safe with one another – not safe from the women, who seemed less of a threat, it was said, than other men. These particular silences seemed to the men who had kept them the expression and enjoyment of mutuality, acceptance and understanding. The silences were a good thing.

One man went on to tell a story of going with his father into the bar of a social club on a caravan site. Sitting at the bar were a collection of men who had known one another for years – standing or leaning or sitting at the bar with their pints, not saying very much. For a while it was very uncomfortable for the visitor, a sense of unwelcome, hostility – or was it just that the men were bored with one another, depressed, utterly inarticulate, half-sozzled? But when there had been time enough to understand the fabric of that situation, this outsider began to appreciate that there was a familiarity, an openness, a mutual comfort in the silence – a kind of shared satisfaction and understanding which he was welcome to join. The silence of just being there in the company of others – a silence which settles, which grows, which may be broken, which may subside and resume and is not imposed or controlling or forbidding or exclusive.

The silences of Christ

Rouault's painting of the silent Christ depicts that we have come to know of God in silence. The Word made flesh is not a spoken revelation only. In flesh the Word becomes silence as well as spoken words. It is not only that which we *heard* who is God, but that which was *seen with our eyes, which we have looked upon and touched with our hands* (I John 1.1ff.), the one who was *beheld*, silently revealed – the one whom the prophet knows to be the Lamb of God simply in his walking, in his presence, in his passing by without words (John 1.35ff.). Christ's humanity is spoken and silent. He is the silent maker of signs as well as the speaker of truth. To know the incarnate God is to know the language of Christ's silences, to interpret their nature, to enjoy the silence of his dwelling among us.

In his book *The Stature of Waiting*, William Vanstone suggested that the handing-over of Jesus – his freely chosen submission to betrayal, arrest, trial and death – reveals an aspect of the divine nature: that the Creator freely becomes the subject of the created, waiting for the multifarious meanings of the world continually to dawn upon himself. Men and women, as bearers of God's image, are not only co-workers and co-creators with God, but also 'fellow-sufferers' with God, waiting upon the world to receive its many meanings. This waiting, no less than the activity of making and doing, is part of the God-given dignity of human beings, and the Christian vision of this 'stature of waiting' is

> an important corrective to the professed and public attitudes of today and to the presuppositions on which they are based – the presupposition that human dignity is preserved only to the extent that man is active in the world, and initiates and creates and earns and achieves.[8]

In a somewhat connected way I wonder whether the silence of Christ is a corrective, not only to the relentless activity of men and to their addiction to work and achievement which might be characterized by the ceaselessness of noise and talk, but also to the nature and function of men's silences. For to follow Christ is to let God who became silent in Christ become silent in us. In him the sinfulness of men's silences may be redeemed and find their true dignity. For the silences of Christ are beautiful, grace full, and they challenge our own. The silences of Christ do not separate nor alienate; they are the silences of Sabbath where men may rest in God's resting, where men may appreciate the goodness of creation in God's gladness – the goodness of their own bodies. They are the silences which draw men away from work: the silences of reflection, appreciation, enjoyment, reward. They are the silences of Shalom, where lion and lamb lie down together with the child, the silence of no more war, of sufficient for all, of knowing as we are known. They are the laddered silences of dream, the ascending and descending silences of angels, the silence when heaven and earth meet. They are the silences of dwelling in God, of being in-dwelt, the silences of Spirit searching depths, the silences of love between three persons who are perfectly one and completely distinct, the silence of a triune unity, the silence which is between people and nations in harmonious relationship. All too easily we talk over Christ's silences. There were the long months of his wordlessness when he swam like a dolphin in the warm sea of his mother's womb. Then there were the silences of his sleeping, feeding, dependent self. Among the works of Eric Gill is a sculpture of the sleeping Christ – Christ not as a slumbering baby, but as a man, his face resting on his hands in a posture where there are no words, no actions, but in the least strenuous of ways, his silent being, his bliss. In the Gospels there are the silences of his transformations – water secretly to wine, bread multiplied, the healings without words which drew the noisy, curious crowds to him, which had them talking of him though he wanted them to know a secret, to pray a secret, to treasure an unspoken thing, something hidden and costly, not fully understood, inexplicable, a pearl of great price. Christ urges those who follow him to keep a silence.

In the Gospels Jesus withdraws to a place by himself. He would find a quiet place, a silent place of prayer, of being with the Father – a time of relationship in silence which nourishes relationships where there are many words needed, feeding the times of action, discussion, dispute, proclamation, announcement. And surely there were also the hours of silence with his friends and followers, the times when words were finished, taking root, and then forming again with new connections, different resonances – shared silences when they were walking along together, silences for growing in understanding, silences for not knowing. There was the silence when he learnt of Lazarus' death and when he looked out over the city – the silences of tears, of grief, of knowing the worst.

We have Christ's silence when the crowd closed in on the woman, when he bent down and drew in the sand, making pictures with free flowing fingers when words of condemnation were hardening like the angry grip of hands round stones. His silence there was not the silence of collusion, which was born out of fear for himself, but the silence of compassion, a silence which listened to the terrified silence of the woman accused – a silence which made an opening among all those

verbose closed, decided minds. In the clamour of that situation
Christ's silence safeguards a quiet place for the possibility of
understanding, empathy, self-examination, for forgiveness in
all that furious congested noise of hate. Christ's words to the
accusers seem to grow out of his silence. Sometimes it is his
silence which makes a space where grace could find a place to
rest.

As we have seen, before Pilate, before those accusers who
do so much talking – all those words of politics, theologies,
administrative strategy – his silence, his saying nothing.
Before the mob, the screaming, shouting, swarming waves of
noise, of hate, of spilling words – the Silent One: 'Behold the
Man'. Behold in him all those who are the victims of hurtful
words. Behold all those who are spoken against. Behold all
those who are the targets of hatred and fear. Behold all those
who stand silent before the spoken cruelties of anger and fear.
Behold the true man, the silent mirror who shows us our
snarling, screaming, hating faces, our verbal violence, the one
who receives upon himself the curses of a fallen language, a
creature named by sinful words. Behold the true man, the
silent image of our true selves: wrongly accused, wrongly con-
demned, misunderstood Word among words.

In the whole of Jesus' passion the Gospel narratives have
Jesus saying so little – no more than a few sentences in all that
questioning, asserting, denying, crying, shouting. On the
cross, in the great act, Jesus speaks no more than a few words.
They are precious words, invaluable words, words of agony
and pain and abandonment and accomplishment. And there
also are his agony and pain beyond words: his cries. But with
these words and cries are the long times of silence. His work
is more than a matter of speech. And with him at the cross the
women, his mother, the beloved disciple – all watching, being
there without words, listening to his words, and to his cries,
and to his silence. Discipleship is more than the business of
words.

This is so with his resurrection, too. What the women find is
an empty tomb, a silent place. The women are in terror of the
silence and of the angel's words which are spoken as they

enter the silence: 'He is not here' – the vision and the message and the promise of the silence, which is experience of the risen Christ. What they must tell the others is of a silence, an absence, an emptiness, which signifies another way of being, which sends them forward, to another place where they shall *see* him. They are given the promise of a resurrected Christ who may be known without words, beyond words, a risen Christ whose recognition at the breaking of the bread brings vanishing: his silence.

What the apostles find after the death of their Lord is silence, and in the silence they begin to remember his words, to fathom his promises. In the silence of the empty tomb, his silence, the words bear fruit; they begin to know what they must tell. The gospel takes root in this resurrection silence. The stories of his resurrection appearances are, initially, encounters without words. The risen Christ of the garden is silent, simply being there where Mary is – not spying, not analysing, not calculating her lack of understanding, not assessing her – but the silence which waits and lets her turn to him, which makes a place for grief and misunderstanding and incomprehension, a place for weeping, for the desire of his body to have expression: a silence which allows the physical and the emotional to meet. A silence which stands with the suffering in their pain and longing and search for understanding.

Then there is his coming among the disciples as they meet in fear and grief: yes Jesus comes and speaks as he speaks to Mary in the garden, but first there is just the coming, his being among them, the silent impact of his presence, his body, his breathing, and only then the words of peace, and his showing them his hands and his side. A silence in which that secret anxious place behind locked doors becomes an open place, a place of discovery and understanding where they may know him and touch his wounds and share his suffering. A silence of life, of peace and trust which brings them together in that place of fear, a silence which unites rather than fractures, which strengthens rather than intimidates.

When Jesus shows himself again by the Sea of Tiberias, he is standing on the shore in the early morning, standing watching them fishing, who knows for how long before he calls to them out in the boats – for hours perhaps standing quietly, minding them. A silence which watches, waits, in which their benefit is found as he discerns their hunger and cold on the water; a practical silence spent making a fire, a quiet of cooking, eating, of them knowing his identity; a silence in which their massive catch of fish becomes for them both sustenance and sign of his presence rather than merely gain.

In a culture of reflexivity such as our own, eager for self-expression and the constant articulation of identity, people are sometimes greedy to possess themselves. There are many voices. Silence seems unproductive. Silence can be forgotten, or may come to seem merely a matter of inarticulacy, or may find itself suspect as a strategy of evasion. At a time when it would seem that religious allegiance must shout out and advertise its services and products in competition with other purveyors of meaning, what is the purpose or benefit of silence in such a market place? Perhaps only that men have done so much talking, and would be glad to discover and deepen their silences, to explore them, transform them, have them redeemed. Silence as part of a different, authentic way of being men.

Yet the silences of Christ encourage men to interrogate their silences and to discern among them those which build bridges and which are barriers, those which promote the abuse of power and the exclusion of others, and those which make places of welcome, rest, peace and acceptance. Which silences allow the cry of the poor and the case of the powerless to be heard? Which silences make a space in the crowd of competing interests for the needs and hurts and separations that demand reconciliation? Which silences are 'deaf' and which are 'hearing'? Which silences discern the silences of others? When men keep silence, and not least the silence of prayer, is this the silence of the inner journey, the silence which takes us outward in love and justice toward 'the other', towards the encounter with God and our fellow human beings? The silences of Christ remind us that our knowing cannot be all words. In the busy-ness of men's search for self-understanding these silences point us forward to that moment of self-knowledge which is gift, beyond us, when we shall fully know ourselves as we are known. Only then shall we see face to face, and the silences of Christ are silences which welcome us to enter into that eternal knowing, to know now that we are known and loved and delighted in, and that the pain and exuberance of our self-discovery as men is spoken in this silence of God's knowing.

For now we see in a mirror dimly, but then face to face. Now I know in part; then I shall understand fully, even as I have been fully understood (I Corinthians 13.12).

9

Seven Meditations on the Sexual Spirit

So God created humankind in his image,
in the image of God he created them;
male and female he created them.

(Genesis 1.27, NRSV)

Born of a Woman
   (Matthew 2.11)

Beneath the mound of his belly
In the valley of his thighs
At source,
Is the tuber
With the two tiny bulbs
Which root and swell in Nazareth, Galilee, Gethsemane's
   garden
Stiffening up into the lush tree of Calvary's Cross.

Minister's Song
   (Luke 18.35–43)

Do not mistake me for the strong one.
The poor man in me
Reaches to the poor man
In you:
Crying child comforting
Crying child.
Together, unseen
We will sit by the side of the road
And watch the fast parts of us
Speeding by
In their smooth, impenetrable cars.

Touching in the Sea
  (Matthew 14.31)

Friday night. It's rained all day. I'm late I know, so by the time I push my way into the bar from the street it's already crammed and I'm drenched inside and out. There's no chance of getting a seat or even making my way to the bar without a struggle through the crowd of drinkers. In the sudden warmth of the pub it feels tropical beneath my layers of clothing. The bar is like a sauna, stuffed with steaming office workers slowly getting sozzled after a long week's work. My spectacles have clouded up into a blur. The noise of frantic conversation and laughter in my ears is like the roar of a deep dive. I've sunk into a sub-oceanic world, a sea of people. They're strange these water creatures. They don't spread themselves around the pub economically, sensibly set out like in their balance sheets, in order. Here they indulge in chaos, they pool together in the central space, touching, swaying into one another, nudging and rubbing and breathing on to one another, smelling end of day perfume and alcoholic breath. Lots of them I know. Sue from personnel is screaming the happenings of office politics to Jan, safe in the roar of all the other screams surrounding them. Those prats Damien and Rod and Ben are ranting about some cock-up made that day, showing their gums and sending themselves hoarse with ruthless, absolute delight in doing someone over. Friday night release.

But no sign of Tom. He's even later than I am! I was hoping to see him up in one of those alcoves, at a table ready with a pint prized out of the impossibly busy bar. Too much to hope for. So I head that way myself, towards the empty seats around the edge on the raised up bit behind the imitation foliage, a pretend terrace, a little beach. Much safer on the shore. I grab a couple of stools and plonk them by the table with my beer on. I shove away the half-eaten roll and empty crisp packets left from lunch-time. I sling the mac across a stool to make it Tom's. Then the first long slug of cold going down my throat is wonderful, and I look toward the door beyond the writhing sea in front of me. Still no sign of Tom.

Jan and Sue are really going at it. No doubt there are serious happenings in their fourth-floor world. Personnel is full of funny goings on. Jan's particularly animated tonight. Her dangly ear-rings are swinging around her neck like they're in some kind of storm as she makes her point to Sue. I can see that Sue is rather taken with the ear-rings too. She stares at them, following their course with her eyes, nodding to Jan to go on talking as they spring about in the current of Jan's head. Sue is admiring them, smiling. She is thinking how beautiful they make Jan's neck with their movements.

Now Sue's eyes are looking back at Jan's. Jan is talking to her, really talking. It strikes me as they stand there how much attention one pays to the other, how much Sue listens as Jan talks, how unafraid of one another they are down in that sea of theirs. Then some great hulking meat-head suited City boy knocks into Sue and sends her stumbling forward. Jan catches her and steadies her to her feet. They laugh and make some joke about the drunk whose hands are full of tippling pints, and Jan's arm stays round Sue's waist beyond the functional time into a moment of caress. She reassures her friend and moves from rescue in to touch.

I am watching two friends touch. There is another wave in the sea of bodies round them. Tom is pushing past, shouting something at me about waking up and getting him a pint. His hair is plastered down by rain, as if by water force. His suit is darkened by the wet. He's grinning like a dolphin in the ocean. I'm diving from my seat. I'm swimming through the people with an impulse to embrace him. I'm walking on the water thrilled to know that for the first time I shall hug him.

The Anointing
  (Mark 14.1–10; Luke 24.13–31)

Now that these smears have shown me
If you follow
Then you shall have the poor with you always.
Not as a burden,
Nor as an issue,
Not merely as a matter of concern,
But walking beside you on the journey
As a friend.

You will not always have me.

Though now you have the outrage of my body for your
    cherishing,
Though now I am here for the clinging
For you to lay your head upon
For the kiss,
Through the kisses' door I shall be gone
And you shall flee naked from the garden of touch
To find your friend
The nameless traveller.

Walking with you in the Way
They shall be with you always
In their bodies,
And they shall be knocking you up in the night
Asking for food
Like friends,
Giving you the grace of doing good
Nourishing justice
When I am gone.
And together
In the breaking of bread
You shall see me
Vanishing.

The Burial
  (John 19.39)

On the edge of evening I make your bed
Deep in a place without light,
Heaving up the slumpen haul of you
To wrap the sheets and resin round
As if to give you shelter from the wind.

No wind in this stone womb,
Only the winding,
The probe of massage
At your breathless form;
My ancient, learned, insufficient ointment spreads
In tests across your flesh to
Pool around the obscene wounds.
Are they the blush of love
Or shame?

This is my second undertaking in the dark:
I found you once before at night,
Heavy then with questions, coming down
The long dim uterine folds of hidden search
From which you tugged me
Into blinding light.
Having seen
Your thrash upon the wood,
Your pain that chased away the sun,
The push and cry and surge and pang
I grope again around the obscure breaking out
Of something new,
Anticipating birth.

Yet not a breath of wind
Nor movement but my own,
Death's midwife – here
To cut the binding cord and tie a knot,

All wonder at your seeping holes.
How can it be that these are openings
To let new traffic in the Spirit
Come and go?

Across the River

On the other side (John 20.11–18)

I sought a lover over the bridge, and in the dark and wet I
found him. The city is in two parts you see, like the brain, and
it was in the other town that he lived, the town across the
river. Down through the damp lands I went on my bike in the
rain, down through the waterlands with my tyres sucking the
path which was stream, a slobber of rubber in wet as the
unseeable sky pumped and writhed the drench all around.
Down I sped to the river as if to an exodus. Like a mad thing I
was that night, desperate, fleeing the broad streets of order
and reason as I surged to the bridge and passed over the river
which quivered its banks to bursting, ecstatic, parting for me.
Crazed, converted, zealous for the cause of him I was, eager
for the finding of him where he is to be found: in his hide, in
his orchard den, his pavilion deep in the vineyard of those
streets as dark and narrow as a secret place of pleasure. There
I found him, a foreign lover.

He is an Arab in the tent of his bed. Desert prince. Bedouin.
Hunter. Like a wanderer in the wilderness he is pitched a
thousand leagues from home, and what a trade he does me
when I journey to him, what lovely barter as we learn the
language of the other in his tabernacle sheets. He is a dancer
in the firelight turning, turning; spirit she is, her fingers
loosening all things as she knows me, names me, plays me, as
she has me swifting in delight with her to speed her sacred
errands on; ah, cook he is to draw me with his stew, such stew;
the bearer of impossible children, how she has me laughing
with her laughter, how she has me hungering to be drawn up
from the well, to be set telling dreams their meanings which
take substance in his presence, at his touch, who makes the

strange land mine, my singing kingdom come with favour of his love.

Tree on the banks of the river he heals me leaf on leaf unfolding peace in parts which raged their wars for years and years unceasing, now at rest, now at love, now the doing of a new thing, barren lands set free in springing spurts of bud – his easter, easter, easter rising like a morning in me, calling me my name from deep within who made my grief his garden, let me tell you how I long to cling to him for ever who has taught me that the fear filled tomb is empty with his life. Let me tell you how I long to cling to him.

> Rabboni, Teacher,
> Let me touch you always.
> Show me your pain.
> Let my fingers know your lordly wound.

In the palace of the hardened heart (Exodus 9–11)

She is a Pharaoh, my mother the bishop, a Governor. She has a grand house befitting her role off an avenue rising up from the river. She strides across the large room of her office with a confidence she does not have. She is not the owner of her attitude, not really, not inside. She does not listen to *inside,* my mother the bishop : she is too busy, too caught up with all the people she has to care for, all the people she has to feed who come to her, all the money she has to find, all the good she has to do, all the protecting. She makes trips across the river, my mother the bishop, missionary trips to the other side. She wants to make it like the town she understands, the town she knows.

So of course she did not realize. Though we sat on the same sofa as a way of saying, she did not hear us. We stood in the big bay window close together and viewed the town below hoping she would do the sums of our space, study the scriptures of our looks, hear the litanies of our laughter, understand. But we were talking different languages, and she was busy, my mother the bishop, getting sorted for her Complementarity Workshop. She tries very hard to take a responsible attitude and to be caring, but she cannot see what is in her own house, my mother the bishop, not even when it stares her in the face and smiles.

What I fear are the plagues of her anger, the rant of her guilt. What I fear when I stand by her fire are the questions: 'Do you know him? Were you with him? Are you another from his country?' What I fear are all the lies we might tell one another in this big house of Truth.

> Ah, holy mother church
> Why do you not listen to your children?
> Why do you cause your little ones to stumble?
> Why do you give them scorpions
> Instead of fish?
> Stones
> When they ask for bread?

Together in one place (Acts 2.1–4)

In the end my mother had to give it up, the Palace. She couldn't afford the repairs; it was impossible to keep warm. We moved into a smaller house. A house across the river. All three of us together.

We are learning one another's language now. I am learning mine, and his, and hers. We can talk to one another, we can listen, understand, converse. There is a commonwealth between us in this little place of ours. And when I lie with him and hear the wind and feel his breath like flame upon my skin saying peace, peace, then I know where heaven is and my mother the bishop is happy for me and for him in this promised land we share across the river.

O Thou Enlightener
Give light
That we may see
Thy works of love
And share Thy joy
In peace.

Sexual Territory
  (Genesis 1.31)

  Living by the cold sea

On winter afternoons at twenty-five minutes past four the sea
is grey and the light is grey. Beyond the window of my room
the world is grey – grey from the nearest beach to the farthest
sky, grey even into the very tightest corner where sea and sky
meet and join into one. A watery grey light in the room. My
hair is grey too. It was not always grey, but now … no, not but:
now my hair is grey.

  I lived here as a boy, and so I know that there have always
been winter afternoons when the light deepens into evening
and then night, as the light is deepening now, greyer and
greyer. I could almost always have told you about winter by
this sea at four twenty-five. I could have drawn a picture,
written a poem, an essay, given you some kind of description
had you asked. If you had said to me at the age of three, or if
you had asked at any time in the fifty or so intervening years.
Tell me, Robert, how would it be looking out at the sea from
the warmth of your room in that house by the beach? How
would it be watching the cold sea in the late afternoon of a
winter's day on the east coast of England – how would that
be?' – I could have told you something approximate to how it
is. I might even have spoken evocatively (as is my way) of the
stillness in the chill air as the light cedes its place to dark in a
kind of sullen surrender (I could have told you), a cessation of
activity along the shore, a handing over to invading forces, a
submission to the spotlight surveillance of the moon which
lurks around the corner of the roof-tops before it parks all
night outside above the sea. I could have said something like
that, even as a child, about day into night by the sea at four
twenty-five in winter.

  But (and here I will allow myself a But), but I should not
have known to say about the grey. Only now I understand the
qualities of grey. Only now would I say something of the grey
which hangs between light and dark, between sky and sea,

between water and sand, between salt and pebbles, between one stone and the next – the grey which is all of these, grey upon grey, the confluence and contrast of greys, the congregations and carnivals of differing greys, the grey moment of grey between one grey and the next at four twenty-five in winter.

I'm not going to rush on and say that grey is universally significant. It's just that now grey has an importance for me which it did not have before. Greyness has become a matter of concern and appreciation now that my hair has become the colour of the sky and the sea in winter. Now that winter evening waves of sea have washed me grey, and grey has seeped into my eyes and coloured them, now I see the miracle and multiplicity of grey – of ordinary mushrooms, their upper greynesses of pockmarked skin, their darker corrugated undersides, a world of grey, grey inside and out. Now I see the loveliness of grey.

And Jane, when she sets the tea tray down on the table in the window, interrupting my view of the sea for a moment, and I watch her hair fall across her face in the movement of her bending, and I see the swerve and current of its greyness, then her loveliness dawns on me. Her grey grey loveliness. Then she passes me my afternoon's consignment of pills with her faint smile, wondering if I'm alright. And I smile back, loving her age – loving mine.

Nowadays, since the illness became so much more debilitating, I sleep for hours after lunch, and then wake to watch the sea again and see the late afternoon light fade, as it is fading now. Sometimes when I open my eyes there are ferries in the far distance, on the horizon, crossing to and fro between The Netherlands and Harwich. Their tiny lights make the grey evening seem like a festival. Sometimes I have dreamed of the illness whilst asleep: in my dream the disease is a kind of grey in my body, a greying inside, but I … . no, no – no buts … in my dream *I love the grey*. In my dream I am able to love the sickness.

And if you were to ask me now to describe for you the winter afternoons I watch from my window, I would take pleasure in telling you the gospel of their greynesses.

The time by the warm sea

I used to sit and watch the ferries, great brilliant white ships which would come round the far edge of the bay and foam up the blue sea with white as they surged into harbour and poured out the cars and the tourists on to the island. I would watch this surge from the terrace on the hillside a long way above the port, and though I could hear nothing of it, I knew that there was noise and busyness in the town as the vehicles nudged their way through the crowds of back-packers and the flock of hoteliers swarming around them, calling and shouting, trying to persuade the tired travellers to a room with shower and breakfast. I knew the acrid stench of petrol from the exhausts and the smell of hot tyres and the dismay of the disgorged tourists and the bad temper of the old women trying to go about their shopping in the hot afternoon beyond sleep. And I would feel glad to be up there in the shade of the olive trees away from all the rancour and uncertainty of the town, watching the shards of sun on the sea and wondering how Spiros was in the bank and if he was beset with kids from Germany and home wanting their money changed in a hurry, and thinking this was paradise with the sun and the blue sea and the blue sky and warmth and olives and the clean smell and firm, heavy feel of my discreet, intelligent, deliberate Greek lover.

None of it was what I had expected when I first saw the rock of the island rise out of the sea, the limewashed houses of the port heaped up with the great bare mountain above. I had anticipated friends, real, local friends, and in time a knowledge of their language and an understanding of their culture. I had come hoping for escape from familiar and jaded things, wanting heat, something different. I had expected love too – well, if not quite expected, then excited by the possibility of someone special and close. But Spiros was a surprise, Maria's rather serious brother come back from university, who would accompany us on our excursions at the weekend. Gradually he became my friend too, and then somehow superseded Maria, and was there with me when she was not, showing me the island and bit by bit letting out his laughter and cleverness and charm, until I found I wanted him, and we were finding our first kiss. I think it was a long time before he came to share the apartment which the company allotted me. To Maria's strange delight and her family's puzzlement, we became – what shall I say – we became connected, we became friends. I remember one old boy who would sit smoking by the quay in the evenings calling Spiros over once. 'You and the English man are friends,' he said, 'You make one world.'

Like the old man I would sit and watch the ferries draw in and draw out across the blue bay, watch the holidaymakers come and go, breathing the warm air, then the cooler air of evening. I would sit way up above the blue bay, on the terrace, remembering different parts of Spiros until I heard the mad wail of his moped winding up the long road of the hillside in the dark. How I loved his warm skin, and his black, black hair shot through with blue.

A place for loving

Please do not misunderstand me when I say that I have fantasies of sailing from this grey sea to the warm island which rises out of the blue water. It is not that I am unhappy growing old or being here with Jane; I have chosen to be in this place with her, and we are happy together. As far as I know we have always been happy ever since we met, give or take a few ups and downs. A very ordinary marriage. I accept that things are as they are – which is why I wonder in my mind about a ferry to the island where my Spiros lives, a journey to that other part of my territory. When I was well I would very often walk along the shingle of this eastern beach and think of the black volcanic sand of the days with Spiros, and walking I would come across some washed-up branch or broken box along the shore and think that it had found its way around the world from the blue bay to these grey beaches. I am sure that the energetic blue sea from around that island warms these cooling grey waters.

Because there is Jane and Spiros and me I know there is one

world, one territory, one ecology of love within, with its special currents and particular climates, one part moderating another. I know of my island of rock sprung up from the earth's core and of my low-lying lands which the waves are washing away – one warm, one cool, both beautiful, both dear to me. And yet it may be that within this territory of mine there are countries of mountains and forests and vast tracts of lakes and valleys which I do not know, and shall never visit, but which are there, each having its place in my particularity.

What I do now as I live by this cold sea is to let the world live itself and seek to cherish it in all its shifting, diverse love-liness. As I die here by this cold sea I am conscious that my hours and days are slipping away like the sand being drawn from the shore to the ocean, wave after wave. In the fluid deep beneath the ferries are currents of the warm and cold and blue-grey waters changing places, swilling sand from one place to another like the movement of the Spirit making journeys to and fro.

Bibliography

Abbott Franklin, *New Men, New Minds*, The Crossing Press 1987

Patrick Arnold, *Wildmen, Warriors, and Kings*, New York: Crossroad
  Publishing Company 1991

Augustine, *Confessions*, translated by Henry Chadwick, Oxford
  University Press 1991

F. J. Balasundaram, 'The Theological Basis of the Decade', *Ecumenical
  Review* 46.2, 1994

Wendy Beckett, *The Gaze of Love*, Marshall Pickering 1993

Robert Bly, *Iron John*, Element Books 1991

A. Brittan, *Masculinity and Power*, Blackwell 1989

H. Brod and M. Kaufman (eds.), *Theorizing Masculinities*, Sage 1994

David Cohen, *Being a Man*, Routledge 1990

R. W. Connell, *Gender and Power*, Polity Press 1987

——*Masculinities*, Polity Press 1995

John Dalrymple, 'Silence', in A. V. Campbell (ed.), *A Dictionary of
  Pastoral Care*, SPCK 1987, 254ff.

Mark Doty, 'Becoming a Meadow', in *My Alexandria*, Jonathan Cape
  1995

Anthony Easthope, *What a Man's Gotta Do*, Paladin 1986

Elisabeth Schüssler Fiorenza, *In memory of Her*, SCM Press 1983

Frieda Fordham, *An Introduction to Jung's Psychology*, Penguin Books
  1991

Matthew Fox, *The Coming of the Cosmic Christ*, New York: Harper and
  Row 1988

Anthony Giddens, *The Transformation of Intimacy*, Polity Press 1992

Herb Goldberg, 'Psychology of Men', in Hunter and Rodney (eds.),

Dictionary of Pastoral Care and Counseling, Abingdon Press 1990, 706ff.

Elaine Graham, *Making the Difference: Gender, Personhood and Theology*, Mowbray 1996

Gustavo Gutierrez, *We Drink From Our Own Wells*, Maryknoll: Orbis Books and SCM Press 1984

K.L. Hagan (ed.), *Women Respond to the Men's Movement*, San Francisco: Pandora 1992

Stanley Hauerwas, *Naming the Silences*, T.& T. Clark 1993

F. Hergott and S. Whitfield, *George Rouault: The Early Years 1903–1920*, Royal Academy 1993

Richard Holloway (ed.), *Who Needs Feminism?*, SPCK 1991

Roger Horrocks, *Masculinity in Crisis*, Macmillan 1994

David Jackson, *Unmasking Masculinity*, Unwin Hyman 1990

Grace Jantzen, *Power, Gender and Christian Mysticism*, Cambridge University Press 1995

Robert A. Johnson, *He: Understanding Masculine Psychology*, San Francisco: Harper 1974

——*Owning Your Own Shadow*, San Francisco: Harper 1991

M. Kaufman (ed.), *Beyond Patriarchy*, Oxford University Press 1987

Sam Keen, *Fire in the Belly*, New York: Bantam Books 1991

Garrison Keillor, *The Book of Guys*, Faber 1993

Brendan Kennelly, *A Time for Voices: Selected Poems 1960–1990*, Bloodaxe 1990

Una Kroll, *Vocation to Resistance: Contemplation and Change*, Darton, Longman and Todd 1995

Björn Krondorfer (ed.), *Men's Bodies, Men's Gods*, New York University Press 1996

Hans Küng (ed.), *Yes To A Global Ethic*, SCM Press 1996

Kenneth Leech, *True Prayer*, Sheldon Press 1980

Liturgical Commission of the Church of England, *Making Women Visible*, Church House Publishing 1989

Ann Loades (ed.), *Feminist Theology: A Reader*, SPCK 1990

Astrid Lobo Gujiwala, 'Women: A New Reality, New Responses', *Vidyajyoti*, LVIII. 12, 1994

Kenneth A. Lockridge, *The Sources of Patriarchal Rage*, New York University Press 1992

Neil Lyndon, *No More Sex War*, Mandarin Books 1992

Roy McCloughry, *Men and Masculinity: From Power to Love*, Hodder & Stoughton 1992

Alistair McFadyen, *The Call To Personhood*, Cambridge University Press 1990

Sally McFague, *The Body of God: An Ecological Theology*, Minneapolis: Fortress Press and SCM Press 1993

Thomas Merton, 'A Letter on the Contemplative Life', in *The Monastic Journey*, ed. Patrick Hart, Sheldon Press 1977

A. Metcalf and M. Humphreys, *The Sexuality of Men*, Pluto 1990

Peter Middleton, *The Inward Gaze*, Routledge 1992

John Milbank, *Theology and Social Theory*, Blackwell 1990

R. Moore and D. Gillette, *King, Warrior, Magician, Lover*, San Francisco: Harper 1990

Blake Morrison, *And When Did You Last See Your Father?*, Granta 1993

James B. Nelson, 'On Men's Liberation', in *Between Two Gardens*, New York: Pilgrim Press 1983

——*The Intimate Connection: Male Sexuality, Male Spirituality*, SPCK 1992

——and Sandra P. Longfellow (eds.). *Sexuality and the Sacred*, Mowbray 1994

Henri Nouwen, *The Return of the Prodigal Son*, Darton, Longman and Todd 1992

Mercy Oduyoye, *Who Will Roll The Stone Away?*, Geneva: WCC Risk Books 1990

Samuel Osherson, *Finding Our Fathers*, New York: Ballatine 1986

Constance Parvey (ed.), *The Community of Women and Men in the Church*, Geneva: Risk Books 1983

John S. Pobee (ed.), *Culture,Women and Theology*, New Delhi: ISPCK 1994

David Porter (ed.), *Between Men and Feminism*, Routledge 1992

Donald Reeves, *Down to Earth: A New Vision for the Church*, Mowbray 1995

M. Roper and J. Tosh (eds.), *Manful Assertions*, London: Routledge 1991

Rosemary Radford Ruether, *Gaia and God*, SCM Press 1995

Lynne Segal, *Slow Motion*, Virago 1990

Victor J. Seidler, *Rediscovering Masculinity*, Routledge 1989

Keith Thompson, *To Be A Man*, Los Angeles:Tarcher 1991

Leo Tolstoy, 'Father Sergius', in *Master Man and Other Stories*, Penguin Books 1977

W. H. Vanstone, *The Stature of Waiting*, Darton, Longman and Todd 1982

Pauline Webb, *She Flies Beyond*, Geneva: Risk Books 1993

Angela West, 'A Faith for Feminists', in *Walking on the Water*, ed. J. Garcia and S. Maitland, Virago 1983

James and Evelyn Whitehead, 'Re-imagining the Masculine', *The Way* 32, 1992, 113–22

E. P. Wimberly, 'The Pastoral Care of Men', in Hunter and Rodway (eds), *Dictionary of Pastoral Care and Counseling*, Nashville: Abingdon Press 1990, 704ff.

Virginia Woolf, *A Room Of One's Own* (1929), Oxford University Press 1994

——*Three Guineas* (1938), Oxford University Press 1992

Brian Wren, *What Language Shall I Borrow? God-Talk in Worship: A Male Response to Feminist Theology*, SCM Press 1989

Notes

Full publication details of books cited in the notes are given in the Bibliography.

Introduction: Listening to the Voice of this Book

1. Kennelly, *A Time for Voices:Selected Poems 1960–1990*, 12.
2. Webb, *She Flies Beyond*, 6.

1. On Learning From Women

1. Woolf, *A Room of One's Own*, 4.
2. Ibid., 31.
3. Ibid., 4.
4. Ibid., 139.
5. Ibid., 114.
6. Ibid., 118.
7. Ibid., 132.
8. Ibid., 133.
9. Woolf, *Three Guineas*, 336ff.
10. Ibid., 309.
11. Ibid., 329.
12. Hearn's paper *Power & Change? Men's Groups, Men's Violences and Managements*, Cambridge Masculinity Seminars 1995.
13. *A Cry of the Beloved*, Methodist Conference 1995.
14. See Section 10 of the Letter in *The Tablet*, 15 July 1995, 919.
15. Ibid., Section 7.

2. On Not Knowing What To Say

1. James B. Nelson's Epilogue to *Men's Bodies, Men's Gods*, ed. Bjorn Krondorfer, 312.
2. Feminist scholarship is uncovering 'lost' traditions of women's voices, and exposing the ways in which men of power have

sought to marginalize and silence women, e.g. Grace Jantzen's *Power, Gender and Christian Mysticism*. Similarly, the work of John Boswell reveals the culture and practise of homosexuality and its repression: *Christianity, Social Tolerance and Homosexuality* and *Same-Sex Unions in Premodern Europe*.
3. From a madrigal c.1538–44 written for Vittoria Colonna, in *The Poetry of Michelangelo*, ed. and trans. James M. Saslow, 305.

3. Men's Voices

1. Cohen, *Being a Man*, 14.
2. In her book *She Flies Beyond: Memories and Hopes of Women in the Ecumenical Movement*, Pauline Webb tells the story of the emergence of women as full participants in the World Council of Churches and the ecumenical process, and the shift from isolating 'women's issues' toward a vision of women and men working together for a new human community.
3. Christopher Rowland in Holloway (ed.), *Who Needs Feminism?*, 62.
4. *Achilles Heel* I, Summer 1978, quoted in Segal, *Slow Motion*, 287.
5. Giddens, *The Transformation of Intimacy*, 30.
6. A process which Foucault summed up thus: 'The sodomite had been an aberration; the homosexual was now a species', quoted in Segal, *Slow Motion*, 136.
7. See Giddens, *The Transformation of Intimacy*, 18ff.
8. Jackson, ix.
9. E.g. the collection of essays by men in *Beyond Patriarchy* (1987), ed. M. Kaufman; and R. W. Connell's *Masculinities* (1995), Part II.
10. Cohen, *Being a Man*, 14–15.
11. Segal, *Slow Motion*, Preface.
12. Middleton, *The Inward Gaze*, 3.
13. Seidler, *Rediscovering Masculinity*,183ff.; or Brittan, *Masculinity and Power*, 198ff.
14. Connell, *Masculinities*, 9.
15. Ibid., 21
16. Middleton, *The Inward Gaze*, 126

4. Rediscovering the Deep Masculine

1. Fordham, *Introduction to Jung's Psychology*, 27.
2. Bly, *Iron John*, xi.
3. Thompson, xvff.

4. Bly, *Iron John*, 6.
5. Ibid., 230.
6. Bly, 'What Men Really Want', in *New Men, New Minds*, ed. Abbott,170.
7. Bly, *Iron John*, 26.
8. Ibid., 249.
9. Keen, *Fire in the Belly*, 6.
10. Ibid., 46.
11. Ibid., 65.
12. Ibid., 72.
13. Ibid., 78.
14. Ibid., 121.
15. Ibid., 192.
16. Ibid., 211.
17. Ibid., 221.
18. Ibid., 217ff.
19. Ibid., 226. Both Keen and Bly give attention to this 'wound' and the importance of it being healed, explored by Osherson, *Finding Our Fathers*.
20. Hagan (ed.), *Women Respond to the Men's Movement*, 17.
21. Ibid., 79.
22. Ibid., Introduction.
23. See David Bartlett's interview with Stoltenberg in *Achilles Heel* II, Summer 1991, 25.
24. Holloway (ed.), *Who Needs Feminism?*, 157ff.
25. See John Archer (ed.), *Male Violence*, Part IV.
26. Hagan (ed.), *Women Respond to the Men's Movement*, 123.
27. Ibid., 124.

5. Reconstructing Men and Masculinity

1. Antonio Gramsci, from his *Prison Notebooks*, quoted by Jackson, *Unmasking Masculinity*, 1.
2. See Hearn and Collinson, 'Theorizing Unities and Differences Between Men & Masculinities', in *Theorizing Masculinities*, ed. Brod and Kaufman, 97ff.
3. Segal, *Slow Motion*, x.
4. Ibid., 72.
5. Easthope, *What a Man's Gotta Do*, 166.
6. Ibid., 6.
7. Connell, *Masculinities*, 76ff.

8. Ibid., 3ff.
9. Ibid., 44.
10. Ibid., 72.
11. Graham, *Making the Difference*, 26.
12. Jackson, *Unmasking Masculinity*, 110.
13. Ibid., 69.
14. Ibid., 94. For a theological reflection on these issues see Reeves, *Down to Earth*, Chapter 8.
15. Osherson, *Finding our Fathers*, 193.
16. Ibid., 229. This is what Bly calls 'making two rooms for the father' within the psyche: one for his 'blessed side', and one for his shadow – see Bly, *Iron John*, 118ff.
17. Osherson, *Finding our Fathers*, 26.
18. Cohen, *Being a Man*, 41.
19. Ibid., 72.
20. Connell, *Masculinities*, 211.
21. Ibid., 241.
22. Ibid., 228.
23. Connell, *Masculinities*, refers to Carole Pateman's observation that 'men exercise power not over a gender but over embodied women, and exercise power as a sex', 230.
24. Ibid., 234.
25. Ibid., 237.
26. See Graham, *Making the Difference*, Chapter 10.
27. Milbank, *Theology and Social Theory*, 5.

6. Behold the Man

1. Daphne Hampson, 'God, Gender and Human Equality', *The Independent*, 13 November 1993.
2. Keen, *Fire in the Belly*, 102.
3. E.g. 'Today a Christology which elevates Jesus' maleness to ontologically necessary significance suggests that Jesus' humanity does not represent women at all. Incarnation solely into the male sex does not include women and so women are not redeemed' (Rosemary Radford Ruether, in *Feminist Theology Reader*, ed. Ann Loades, 138ff.).
4. Keillor, *The Book of Guys*, 10.
5. Moore and Gillette, *King, Warrior, Magician, Lover*, xviii.
6. Arnold, *Wildmen, Warriors, and Kings*, 200ff.
7. Ibid., 181ff.

8. Ibid., 199.
9. Ibid., 184.
10. Nelson, *Between Two Gardens*, 39.
11. Ibid., 54.
12. Nelson, *The Intimate Connection*, 107.
13. Ibid., 108.
14. Ibid., 89.
15. Ibid., 100.
16. Ibid., 103.
17. Ibid., 107.
18. Ibid., 110.
19. McCloughry, *Men and Masculinity*, 133.
20. Ibid., 135, drawing on Pleck's *The Myth of Masculinity*.
21. Ibid., 137.
22. Ibid., 140.
23. Ibid., 141.
24. Ibid., 256.
25. Quoted in ibid., 139.
26. Angela West, 'A Faith for Feminists', in *Walking on the Water*, ed. J.Garcia and S. Maitland, 89.
27. McCloughry, *Men and Masculinity*, 142.
28. Wren, *What Language Shall I Borrow?*, 188ff.
29. Whitehead, 'Re-imagining the Masculine', 116.
30. Ibid., 121.

7. *Imagining Ways of Being Together*

1. St Augustine, *Confessions*, Book V. i.
2. Doty, 'Becoming a Meadow', in *My Alexandria*, 63. Used by permission.
3. Iris Murdoch, *The Sublime and the Good*, quoted McFague, *The Body of God*, 50.
4. Murdoch, from *The Sovereignty of Good*, quoted ibid., 49.
5. Ibid., 211.
6. Stephen Jay Gould, *The Flamingo's Smile*, quoted ibid., 197.
7. Ibid., 198.
8. See McFague, Chapter 6; Radford Ruether's *Gaia & God*, and Matthew Fox's *The Cosmic Christ*.
9. McFadyen, *The Call to Personhood*, 31.
10. Ibid., 42ff.
11. Ibid., 9.

12. See Küng (ed.), *Yes To A Global Ethic*, and Reeves, *Down to Earth* (1995).
13. Gutierrez, *We Drink From Our Own Wells*, 134.

8. On Silence

1. Jantzen, *Power, Gender and Christian Mysticism*, 346.
2. Merton, from 'A Letter on the Contemplative Life', *The Monastic Journey*, 173.
3. See also Luke 23.8ff.; Mark 15.1ff.; Matt. 27.11ff.; John 19.1ff.
4. Wendy Beckett, *The Gaze of Love*, 10.
5. Merton, 'A Letter on the Contemplative Life', 171. This is what Sr Wendy Beckett refers to as facing our 'unreality' in prayer: *The Gaze of Love*, 10.
6. Merton, 'A Letter on the Contemplative Life', 172.
7. As told to Rajneesh Dham, *Delhi Sunday Observer*, 1 January 1995.
8. Vanstone, *The Stature of Waiting*, 109.